Anonymous

The Southern Soldier's Prize Songster

Containing martial and patriotic pieces (chiefly original), applicable to the

present war

Anonymous

The Southern Soldier's Prize Songster
Containing martial and patriotic pieces (chiefly original), applicable to the present war

ISBN/EAN: 9783337309251

Printed in Europe, USA, Canada, Australia, Japan

Cover: Foto ©ninafisch / pixelio.de

More available books at **www.hansebooks.com**

THE

SOUTHERN SOLDIER'S

PRIZE SONGSTER,

Containing Martial and Patriotic Pieces,
(CHIEFLY ORIGINAL,)
Applicable to the present war.

MOBILE, ALA:
W. F. WISELY, NO. 33, ST. MICHAEL ST.
1864.

PREFATORY.

A COLLECTION of the metrical effusions of Southern genius, elicited by the present war, is a desideratum in the Confederacy. Many Song Books have been issued to supply the great demand for that species of literature in our Army, but they have been almost exclusively collections of European or Yankee lyrics, illy suited, if not adverse, to the spirit and purposes of our people. This is not just, either to the capacities or the demands of the country. The glorious cause in which the South is struggling, is well calculated to call forth the highest manifestations of intellect and enthusiasm, and to give birth to those fervid sentiments—those "thoughts that breathe and words that burn," which have characterized her gifted sons in every department of feeling, eloquence or song.

Thinking thus, the publisher of the present volume, determined to use his efforts to produce a collection of original Songs, solely by Southern writers, which should be creditable to the heart and mind of our country, and help to inspire those lofty sentiments which are the very soul of patriotism and military valor. The Songs of a nation, as illustrated in the Marseilles Hymn, Rule Britannia, and other kindred gems, are as potent as her arms in protecting her against tyranny and aggression.

The publisher accordingly offered a premium of FIFTY DOLLARS for the best Song, suited to the present time. A committee of three gentlemen, (Rev. Dr. Pierce, Hon. Percy

Walker and G. Y. Overall, Esq.,) were appointed to make the award. Near thirty pieces were submitted in competition, most of them possessing high literary merit. After much deliberation, the committee selected the piece entitled "Southland," as the most meritorious. The author's name was not given, he only requesting in his note that the money, if awarded him, should be paid over for the benefit of our necessitous soldiers. This modesty will add to the attractiveness of his piece, which is the first in the present volume.

Numerous original songs have been kindly contributed, since the printing commenced. They constitute a larger mass of native lyrics and ballads than has hitherto been issued in the Confederacy; and will, it is trusted, redound to our intellectual reputation abroad.

Besides the original matter, selections of the best pieces of a kindred character, from periodicals, have been made, so as to present specimens of the talent of most of our Southern writers.

For the elevated purpose which the publisher had in view, and the varied merits of its contents, he trusts that this little volume will meet with popular favor, especially in our gallant Army.

INDEX.

The Pieces Marked with a Star (*) are Original in this Book

A Chant*		103
A Cry to Arms	By Henry Timrod	51
All Quiet along the Potomac	Lamar Fontaine	99
Annie of the Vale*	Paul Pelby	59
Approach of Battle*		40
Arm for the Southern Land	M. B. Lamar	79
Ashby	John R. Thompson	45
Battle Call*	Arthur Belton	75
Blue Cross*	A. B. Meek	25
Cavaliers of Dixie*	B. F. Porter	77
Clocknaben*	Arthur Belton	75
Drummer Boy of Shiloh		62
Dying Soldier*	J. A. Mecklin	14
Farewell*	R. B. Trimmier	43
Forrest's Battle Chorus*	Reuben Nason	44
Gallant Soldier Boy*	Paul Pelby	84
Georgia	Jacques Journot	60
God our Refuge*		102
God Save the South*	Reuben Nason	82
Hymn for Fast Day*		100
Hymn to the Dawn	A. J. Requier	83
I would be a Soldier Still		74
Jefferson Davis*	A. B. Meek	80
John Pelham	James R. Randall	22
Lament for Mumford*	Miss J. M. Porter	41
Land of My Fathers*	A. B. Meek	56
Lifting of the Banner*	A. B. Meek	35
Lone Star Flag	H. L. Flash	53

INDEX.

Louisiana		73
Missouri*	A. Alexander	71
Mobile Banner Song*	Reuben Nason	15
My Love and I	Asa Hartz	63
My Maryland	James R. Randall	66
My Soldier Boy	L. E. Grayson	34
My Wife and Child	H. R. Jackson	59
Not Doubtful of your Fatherland	W. G. Simms	17
Our Country's Ensign*	"Southland"	49
Our Country's Heroes*	A. B. Meek	9
Our Faith	A. J. Requier	30
Post of Danger	M. B. Lamar	94
Re-enlistment	Mrs. M. J. Canedo	28
Re-Enlisted for the War*	M. W. Chapman	22
Richmond on the James	G. E. Burgess	27
Sea-Kings of the South	E. C. B.	54
Seventy-Six and Sixty-one*	J. W. Overall	13
Soldier's Heart*	F. P. Beaufort	58
Southland*	(Prize Song)	7
Southern Cross	St. George Tucker	97
Southern Land*	Evan Elbert	23
Southern Maiden's Valentine*	Mrs. M. J. Canedo	47
Star of Alabama*	A. B. Meek	72
Stonewall Jackson's Way		60
Sumter	Miss E. C. Sloman	85
Tennessee	B. N. Berryhill	86
The Soldier's Last Bugle		104
To the Rescue, Alabama	A. B. Meek	90
Try Us	Francis Baker	48
Uniform of Gray*	Evan Elbert	37
Valiant Conscript		92
Victory	F. P. Beaufort	88
War Child	Anderson	64
Yankee-Doodle-doo*	Alabamian	19

THE
Soldier's Prize Songster.

SOUTHLAND.

THE PRIZE SONG.

They sing of the East.
With its flowery feast,
And clime of the North, with its mountains of snow;
But give me the land
Where the breezes blow bland,
O'er realms of magnolia and myrtle below.
      The land of the South,
      The fair sunny South,
      The flower-crowned South.
      In its *grandeur* for me!

Her sons are aye brave.
And no chains can enslave,
Though countless the hordes of their foemen may be;
    Ah! see, even now,
    As with battle-stained brow,
They vanquish the Northmen on land and on sea!
      The land of the South,
      The young gallant South,

The invincible South,
In its *valor* for me!

Her daughters are fair
As the pure lilies there,
And cheer her brave soldiers for freedom to die;
Their smiles are the light
Of the war-clouded night,
Their tears are sweet dew-drops distilled from the sky.
The land of the South,
The sweet rosy South,
The starry-gemmed South,
In its *beauty* for me!

In green blossomed dales,
And in violet vales,
And fields white with cotton, its dwellings once stood;
The spoilers now seek
Their vile vengeance to wreak,
And darken this Eden with ashes and blood.
The land of the South,
The opulent South,
The long-plundered South,
In its *richness* for me!

Oh, who would not stand
With his life in his hand,
To shield such a land from the feet of the foe?
God made it thus free,
And oh, perish must we.

-Before it can be in bondage laid low!
    The land of the South,
    The proud sovereign South,
    The God-shielded South,
    In its *freedom* for me!

OUR COUNTRY'S HEROES.

BY A. B. MEEK.

Come sing our country's heroes,
  The true and stalwart band,
Whose arms, on many a foughten field,
  Have saved our struggling land;
Who dauntless go to meet the foe,
  Alike on land or sea,—
Three cheers for Bragg and Johnson,
  For Beauregard and Lee!

They left their quiet homesteads,
  Their children and their wives;
They heard their outraged country bid
  Them shield her with their lives;
They saw on high her standard fly
  Amid the battle smoke,—
Three cheers for Hill and Longstreet,
  For Breckinridge and Polk!

They scorned all base submission,
  All weak and coward pleas;
They only heard the trump and drum

Pulsating on the breeze.
They dashed away, and in the fray,
  Like red wine, poured their blood,—
Three cheers for Price and Buckner,
  For Ewell, Cheatham, Hood!

Oft in the hour of carnage,
  We've seen their gallant forms
Bear down upon the foeman's lines.
  Like thunder-bolts in storms.
They heeded not the shell or shot.
  They scorned to pause or flee,—
Three cheers for Smith and Loring,
  Magruder and Hardee!

We'll go where'er they lead us.
  With them no foe we fear,
Their lofty presence, in the fight.
  The weakest heart can cheer.
O'er rolling drum and shrieking bomb,
  Ring out their clarion tones,—
Three cheers for Taylor, Withers,
  For Cleburne, Stuart, Jones!

See, 'mid the rushing squadrons.
  How gallantly they bear!
What light beams from each fearless face!
  How calm and firm they are!
Long lines of steel around them wheel,
  Like planets round the sun,—

Three cheers for Evans, Early.
  For Rodes and Anderson!

We cannot fail to conquer
  With such devoted braves :
Though all the North should come at once,
  We'll give them only—graves!
We'll meet their hordes with trenchant swords,
  Uplifted for our cause,—
Three cheers for Jackson, Clayton.
  For Forney and McLaws!

Old Rome may boast her Scipios,
  And Greece, Miltiades ;
And England tell how Nelson fell
  On rich historic seas.
Let France display Murat and Ney,
  Our battle trump replies,—
Three cheers for Morgan, Forrest.
  For Chalmers, Wheeler, Wise!

The Yankee soldiers tremble
  Whene'er they hear their names,—
They've seen their chargers spurn the earth,
  Amid the sulphur flames!
They sneak away in search of prey,
  And plunder, burn and rob,—
Three cheers for Adams, Maury.
  For Finnegan and Cobb!

Oh, many a verdant garland

Shall maiden fingers twine,
To wreathe around the scar-seamed brows
Of that illustrious line.
The roll of fame shall show each name,
Engirt with golden rays,—
Three cheers for Pickett, Parsons,
For Gracie, Hindman, Deas!

Lo! on the storm-swept ocean,
We've lion spirits too,
Who've snatched the sceptre of the seas.
From many a Yankee crew.
Their iron fleet, though clad complete,
In constant terror swims,—
Three cheers for brave Buchanan,
Farrand, Lynch, Maffit, Semmes!

Then sing our country's heroes,
We cannot name them all,—
They're found on every crimson field,
Prompt to their country's call.
In deathless verse, bards shall rehearse
Their praise through future time,—
Three cheers then for our heroes,
And for their deeds sublime!

SEVENTY-SIX AND SIXTY-ONE.*

BY JOHN W. OVERALL.

Ye spirits of the glorious dead!
  Ye watchers in the sky!
Who sought the patriot's crimson bed
  With holy trust and high—
Come lend your inspiration now,
  Come fire each southern son,
Who nobly fights, for freemen's rights,
  And shouts for sixty-one.

Come teach them how on hill, in glade,
  Quick leaping from your side,
The lightning flash of sabres made
  A red and flowing tide:
How well ye fought, how bravely fell,
  Beneath our burning sun,
And let the lyre, in strains of fire,
  So speak of sixty-one.

There's many a grave in all the land,
  And many a crucifix,
Which tell how that heroic band
  Stood firm in seventy-six—
Ye heroes of the deathless past,
  Your glorious race is run,
But from your dust, springs freemen's trust,
  And blows for sixty-one.

*The era of Southern Confederate Independence.

We build our altars where you lie
   On many a verdant sod,
With sabres pointing to the sky,
   And sanctified of God—
The smoke shall rise from every pile,
   Till freedom's fight is done,
And every mouth throughout the South,
   Shall shout for sixty-one.

THE DYING SOLDIER.

BY JAMES A. MECKLIN.

Gather round him where he's lying,
   Hush your footsteps, whisper low,
For a soldier here is dying,
   In the sunset's radiant glow.

Beating, beating, slowly beating,
   Runs the life-blood through his frame;
Swift the soldier's breath is fleeting,
   And he calls his mother's name:

"Mother, mother, come and kiss me,
   Ere my spirit fades away,
For I know you oft will miss me,
   When you watch the sinking day.

"Brother, sister, nearer, nearer!
   Place, oh, place your hands in mine,

You, whose love than life was dearer.
  Let your arms around me twine.

"Father, see, the sun is fading
  From the hill-tops of the west,
And the valley night is shading—
  Farewell, lov'd ones, I'm at rest."

Dying, dying! yes, he's dying;
  Close the eyelids, let him rest;
No more sorrow, no more sighing,
  E'er again shall heave his breast.

Sleeping, sleeping, calmly sleeping,
  In the church-yard cold and drear,
And the wintry winds are heaping
  O'er him leaflets brown and sear;

And he's resting, where forever
  Clang of trumpet, roll of drum,
Roar of cannon, never, never,
  Never more to him shall come.

MOBILE BANNER SONG.

BY REUBEN NASON.

Air—"*Red, White and Blue.*"

A song for the land that we honor,
  The clime of the noble and brave,

For the States which support our proud banner
   And our home by the bright-glancing wave.
Her sons in the hour of danger
   Are true as their bayonets' steel,
And their flag is still freedom's avenger.
   Borne on by the lads of Mobile.

Oh, the South is the pride of all nations;
   Heaven smiles on these wide, fertile plains,
And crowns with its richest creations
   A land that shall never know chains.
Her warriors will live to defend her.
   Or on her loved bosom lie low.
While their flag carries victory before it.
   And death to the treacherous foe.

So here's to the land that we cherish.
   The loveliest region of earth;
May all the base hirelings perish
   Who dare to dishonor its worth.
Then, Peace, spread thy pinions—while loudly
   We welcome with jubilant peal
The banner of victory, proudly
   Borne home by the lads of Mobile

NOT DOUBTFUL OF YOUR FATHERLAND.

BY W. GILMORE SIMMS.

Not doubtful of your fatherland,

                                    and

                                    rdes!

                                    oak;

The virtue to maintain it;
The soul to brave, the will to do—
These seek the fight and gain it!
The precious prize
Before your eyes,

The Conquered Banner.

BY FATHER ABRAM J. RYAN, THE POET PRIEST OF THE SOUTH.

Furl that banner, for 'tis weary,
Round its staff 'tis drooping dreary;
 Furl it, fold it, it is best:
For there's not a man to wave it,
And there's not a sword to save it,
And there's not one left to lave it,
In the blood which heroes gave it,
And its foes now scorn and brave it—
 Furl it, hide it, let it rest.

Take that banner down—'tis tattered,
Broken is its staff and shattered
And the valiant hosts are scattered,
 Over whom it floated high.
Oh! 'tis hard for us to fold it,
Hard to think there's none to hold it,
Hard that those who once unrolled it
 Now must furl it with a sigh.

Furl that banner, furl it sadly—
Once ten thousands hailed it gladly,
And ten thousands wildly, madly,
 Swore it should forever wave:
Swore that foeman's sword could never
Hearts like theirs intwined dissever,
Till that flag would float forever
 O'er their freedom or their grave.

Furl it! for the hands that grasped it,
And the hearts that fondly clasped it,
 Cold and dead are lying low:
And the banner, it is trailing,
While around it sounds the wailing
 Of its people in their woe.
For, though conquered, they adore it,
Love the cold, dead hands that bore it,
Weep for those who fell before it,
Pardon those who trailed and tore it,
And oh! wildly they deplore it,
 Now to furl and fold it so.

Furl that banner! true, 'tis gory,
Yet 'tis wreathed around with glory,
And 'twill live in song and story.
 Though its folds are in the dust:
For its fame on brightest pages,
Penned by poets and by sages,
Shall go sounding down the ages,
 Furl its folds though now we must.
Furl that banner, softly, slowly,
Treat it gently—it is holy—
 For it droops above the dead;
Touch it not, unfold it never,
Let it droop there, *furled* forever.
 For its people's *hopes* are dead.

NOT DOUBTFUL OF YOUR FATHERLAND.

BY W. GILMORE SIMMS.

Not doubtful of your fatherland,
  Nor of the God who gave it,
On, Southrons! 'gainst the hireling band
  That struggle to enslave it.
    Ring boldly out
    Your battle shout;
Charge fiercely 'gainst those felon hordes!
    One hour of strife
    Is freedom's life,
And glory hangs upon your swords!

A thousand mothers' matron eyes,
  Wives, sisters, daughters weeping,
Watch, when your virgin banner flies
  To battle, fiercely weeping.
    Though science fails,
    The steel prevails,
With hands that wield our hearts of oak;
    These, though the wall
    Of stone may fall,
Grow stronger with each hostile stroke.

The faith that feels its cause is true,
  The virtue to maintain it;
The soul to brave, the will to do—
  These seek the fight and gain it!
    The precious prize
    Before your eyes,

The all that life conceives of charm,
  Home, freedom, life,
  Child, sister, wife,
All rest upon your soul and arm!

And what the foe, the felon race
  That seek your subjugation?
The scum of Europe, her disgrace,
  The lepers of the nation!
    And what the spoil
    That tempts their toil,
The bait that lures them on to fight?
    Lust, crime and blood,
    Each fiendish mood,
That prompts and follows appetite.

Shall such prevail, and shall you fail,
  Asserting cause so holy?
With souls of might, go seek the fight,
  And crush these wretches lowly.
    On, with the cry,
    To "do or to die,"
As did, in darker days, your sires;
    Nor stay the blow
    'Till every foe,
Down stricken in your path, expires!

YANKEE-DOODLE-DOO!

BY AN ALABAMIAN.

Curse on the canting, whining race,
    The peddling, meddling crew,
Whose hearts are vile, and spirits base,
    And backs and bellies blue!
They brag, they lie, they cheat, they steal,
    In every place and time;
Their souls are bloat with bigot zeal,
    And crusted o'er with crime!
A curse upon their menial crew,
The sniffling, whittling Yankee-doodle-doo!

They've been the pest of all the world,
    Since Cromwell's bloody days;
From Holland's quagmires they were hurled,
    For their pragmatic ways.
The Mayflower ship, that brought them o'er,
    Conveyed a felon flock,
And spewed the vermin on the shore,
    By Plymouth's "blarney rock."
Then curse the Puritanic crew,
The ranting, canting, Yankee-doodle-doo!

In Northern snows their souls congealed
    To ice lumps in their breasts;
Their hearts became like *ing-uns* peeled,
    And by the devil possessed.
Each mother's son, ere he could run,
    His daddy learned to cheat,

And thus a graduate become,
    With peddlers to compete!
Then curse upon the pilfering crew,
The shuffling, snuffling, Yankee-doodle-doo!

They swarmed, like bilge-flies, thro' the land,
    With saintly, drawling speech;
They claimed to be God's missioned band,
    To edit, teach and preach!
With wooden nutmegs, saw-dust seed,
    And pinchbeck ware, they strayed,
And made even little *niggers* " bleed,"
    When they could "strike a trade."
Then curse upon the cheating crew,
The peddling, meddling, Yankee-doodle-doo!

You know them by their coffin face,
    Their pallid lanthern jaws,
Their smirking lips, their sneaking ways,
    Their clumsy feet and paws!
With hypocritic eyes they leer,
    And sycophantic smile;
With nasal twang they utter prayer,
    And rob the church the while!
Then curse the pharisaic crew,
The kneeling, stealing, Yankee-doodle-doo!

They'd filch a bible from a priest,
    But leave a *tract* instead;
The widow's mite they've often seized,
    And ta'en the orphan's bread.

They've got a Bible of their own,
    An Abolition God;
Ward Beecher fills the Savior's throne,
    And Lincoln wields his rod!
Then curse upon the heathen crew,
The robbing, jobbing, Yankee-doodle-doo!

They're cowards in their hollow hearts,
    Nor dare an equal field;
In battle, on their hinder-parts,
    They wisely put the shield;
With iron ship, and long, long gun,
    They keep beyond our shots;
Get near, and every mother's son
    In double quick-time trots!
Then curse upon the dastard crew,
The shunning, running, Yankee-doodle-doo!

Soon from our land we'll drive them all,
    To their dark holes afar;
Thank God! we've broke the Northern thrall,
    And see the rising star!
Yes, Yankee-doodle-doodle-doo,
    We've done with you at last;
Go eat your onions, spin and spew,
    Your " occupation's " passed!
Yet curse upon your cringing crew,
Poor shrieking, sneaking, Yankee-doodle-doo!

JOHN PELHAM.

BY JAMES R. RANDALL.

Just as the spring came laughing thro' the strife,
 With all its gorgeous cheer,
In the bright April of historic life,
 Fell the great cannoneer.

The wondrous lulling of a hero's breath
 His bleeding country weeps—
Hushed in the alabaster arms of death,
 Our young Marcellus sleeps.

Nobler and grander than the child of Rome,
 Curbing his chariot steeds,
The knightly scion of a Southern home
 Dazzled the land with deeds.

Gentlest and bravest in the battle's brunt,
 The champion of the truth,
He bore his banner to the very front
 Of our immortal youth.

A clang of sabres 'mid Virginian snow,
 The fiery pang of shells—
And there's a wail of immemorial woe
 In Alabama's dells.

The pennon droops that led the sacred band
 Along the crimson field;
The meteor blade sinks from the nerveless hand
 Over the spotless shield.

We gazed and gazed upon that beauteous face,
    While 'round the lids and eyes,
Couched in their marble slumber, flashed the grace
    Of a divine surprise.

Oh, mother of a blessed soul on high,
    Thy tears may soon be shed—
Think of thy boy with princes of the sky,
    Among the Southern dead.

How must he smile on this dull world beneath,
    Fevered with swift renown—
He, with the martyr's amaranthine wreath,
    Twining the victor's crown!

SOUTHERN LAND.

BY EVAN ELBERT.

AIR—*Dixie.*

Soldiers, rise and form for battle!
Hark, the deadly cannon's rattle!
Listen now! listen now! listen now! Southern Land!
Lo, across your northern border,
Comes in force the grim marauder!
Rouse up, then! rouse up, then! rouse up, then! Southern Land!

CHORUS—Lift up your lilly banner!
    Hurra! hurra!
    Around it stand, with stalwart band,
    Linked heart and haud, for freedom!
Hurra! hurra! hurra, my gallant Southrons!
Hurra! hurra! hurra, my dauntless Southrons!

Comes he now, with bandit legions,
   Laying waste your fertile regions!
Gather, then! gather, then! gather, then! Southern Land!
   See, his "Stars and Stripes" are gleaming!
   Hark, his vulture-eagle's screaming!
Rally now! rally now! rally now! Southern Land!
      CHORUS—Lift up your lilly banner, &c.

Long you bent, with tame submissionn,
   To the hordes of Abolition!
Waken now! waken now! waken now! Southern Land!
   By your wrongs, and homesteads plundered!
   By the bonds of union sundered!
Meet the foe! meet the foe! meet the foe! Southern Land!
      CHORUS—Lift up your lilly banner, &c.

Do your hearts still feed the fires
   Freedom-lighted by your sires?
Kindle, then! kindle, then! kindle, then! Southern Land!
   Let the flame flash on your altars!
   Curse upon the slave that falters!
Cast him out! cast him out! cast him out! Southern Land!
      CHORUS—Lift up your lilly banner, &c.

By your hills and fields and waters!
   By your mothers, wives and daughters!
Battle now! battle now! battle now! Southern Land!
   Hurl, as did the lordly Roman,
   From your breast, the impious foeman!
Hurl him back! hurl him back! hurl him back! Southern Land
      CHORUS—Lift up your lilly banner, &c.

Now I hear your heroes shouting,
   Where the tyrant they are routing!

Bravely done! bravely done! bravely done! Southern Land!
 Long they'll wear, in song and story,
  Chaplets of unfading glory!
Honor them! honor them! honor them! Southern Land!
  CHORUS--Lift up your lilly banner, &c.

THE BLUE CROSS.

BY A. B. MEEK.

The Blue Cross on its field of red,
 Embossed with golden stars,
Gleams proudly o'er the patriot's head,
 Above the cloud of wars.
It shines on high—lit from the sky—
 The symbol of our faith,
To cheer the band who nobly stand
 For liberty or death!
Oh, comrades, then exulting spread
The Blue Cross on its field of red!

That Cross has shone on many a field
 Where hero-hearts have bled;
Where mighty armies rocked and reeled,
 And piled the earth with dead.
'Mid clashing drums and shrieking bombs,
 The dying turned his eye,
To see it wave above the brave,
 Victoriously on high!
Oh, comrades, then exulting spread
The Blue Cross on its field of red!

O'er leaguered towns and castled walls,
    It flings defiance forth :
In vain your mortars, shells, and balls,
    Oh, grim and baffled North !
That flag still gleams, aye, proudly streams,
    In morning's silvery air,
And through the night, the bomb-shell's light
    Beholds it blazing there !
Oh, comrades, then exulting spread
The Blue Cross on its field of red !

On ocean's broad and brawny breast,
    Where long our foes held sway,
Despite blockades, with fearless crest,
    We now that Cross display !
Proud and serene, its stars have seen
    The conquered ship go down :
Whole navies fear, when it is near,
    And fly before its frown !
Oh, comrades, then exulting spread
The Blue Cross on its field of red !

God grant that heaven-illumined Cross,
    Like Constantine's, may glow,
Until our loved Confederate cause
    Shall conquer every foe ! *

---
* The standard Constantine adopted from a cross he saw in the sky, bore this motto, "*In hoc signs vinces.*"

Its glorious light shall then beam bright,
Through endless ages on,
And this young land the happiest stand
Beneath the sun's blue zone!
Oh, comrades, then exulting spread
The Blue Cross on its field of red!

RICHMOND ON THE JAMES.

BY G. T. BURGESS.

A soldier of our army lay gasping on the field,
When battle's shock was over and the foe was forc'd to yield,
He fell, a youthful hero, before the foeman's aims,
On a blood-red field near Richmond, near Richmond on the James.

But one still stood beside him, his comrade in the fray,
They had been friends together through boyhood's happy day,
And side by side had struggled on field of blood and flames,
To part that eve near Richmond, near Richmond on the James.

He said, "I charge thee, comrade, the friend in days of yore,
Of the far, far distant dear ones that I shall see no more.
Tho' scarce my lips can whisper their dear and well-known names,
To bear to them my blessing from Richmond on the James.

"Bear my good sword to my brother, and the badge upon my breast,
To the young and gentle sister that I used to love the best;
But one lock from my forehead give the mother still that dreams,
Of her soldier boy near Richmond—near Richmond on the James.

"Oh, I wish that mother's arms were folded round me now,
That her gentle hand could linger one moment on my brow,
But I know that she is praying where our blessed hearth-light gleams,
For her soldier's safe return from Richmond on the James.

"And on my heart, dear comrade, close lay those nut-brown braids,
Of one that was the fairest of all our village maids ;
We were to have been wedded, but death the bridegroom claims,
And she is far, that loves me, from Richmond on the James.

" Oh, does the pale face haunt her, dear friend, that looks on thee?
Or is she laughing, singing in careless. girlish glee?
It may be she is joyous, and loves but joyous themes,
Nor dreams her love lies bleeding near Richmond on the James.

"And though I know, dear comrade, thou'lt miss me for awhile,
When their faces—all that lov'd thee—again on thee shall smile ;
Again thou'lt be the foremost in all their youthful games,
But I shall lie near Richmond—near Richmond on the James."

And far from all that loved him, that youthful soldier sleeps,
Unknown among the thousands of those his country weeps ;
But no higher heart nor braver, than his, at sunset's beams,
Was laid that eve near Richmond—near Richmond on the James.

The land is filled with mourning, from hall and cot left lone,
We miss the well-known faces that used to greet our own;
And long poor wives and mothers shall weep, and titled dames,
To hear the name of Richmond—of Richmond on the James.

RE-ENLISTMENT.

BY MARGARITA J. CAÑEDO.

What! shall we now throw down the blade,
  And doff the helmet from our brows?
Now see our holy cause betrayed,
  And recreant prove to all our vows?
When first we drew these patriot swords,
  "A nation's freedom!" was the cry:

Our faith was pledged in these proud words,
  And Heaven has sealed the oath on high.

Since then on dear-bought battle-plains
  We've seen our martyr-brethren die,
While on the soil that drank those stains—
  Their native earth where now they lie,
The foe now treads—th' exulting foe,
  And desecrates the hero-graves.
Say, can we peace or honor know
  While *there* the accursed banner waves?

Dear are our homes, that smile afar;
  Oft in the weary soldier's dreams,
While resting from the toils of war,
  He sees the light that round them beams.
Dear are the loved and lovely maids
  Shrined in the patriot soldier's heart:
Yet, while the foe our land invades,
  In vain the longing tear may start.

No! let the despot's hireling band,
  Who feel not honor—know not faith,
Who war not for their native land,
  Fly trembling from a dreaded death.
Our lives are to our country pledged,
  Until her last red field is won;
For "liberty or death" is waged
  The war where fights her faithful son.

Then plant that flag-staff in the earth,
  And round it rally, every son

Who loves the State that gave him birth,
　Till her proud sovereignty be won.
What though our limbs be weak with toil,
　What though we bear full many a scar;
Huzza! here's to our native soil,
　We re-enlist, and for the war!

OUR FAITH.

BY A. J. REQUIER.

Not yet one hundred years have flown
　Since, on this very spot,
The subjects of a Sovereign throne—
　Liege-masters of their lot,
This high decree sped o'er the sea.
　From council-board and tent,
" No earthly power can rule the free
　But by their own consent!"

For this they fought as Saxons fight,
　On bloody fields and long—
Themselves the champions of the right
　And judges of the wrong;
For this their stainless knighthood wore
　The branded rebel's name,
Until the starry cross they bore
　Set all the skies aflame!

And States co-equal and distinct
　Outshone the Western sun,

The Ashes of Glory.
BY A. J. REQUIER.

Fold up the gorgeous silken sun,
    By bleeding martyrs blest,
And heap the laurels it has won
    Above its place of rest.

No trumpet's note need harshly blare,
    No drum funereal roll,
Nor trailing sables drape the bier
    That frees a dauntless soul.

It lived with Lee and decked his brow
    From fate's empyreal palm;
It sleeps the sleep of Jackson now,
    As spotless and as calm.

It was outnumbered, not undone—
    And they shall shuddering tell
Who struck the blow. Its latest gun
    Flashed rain as it fell.

Sleep, shrouded ensign! Not the breeze
    That smote the victor tar
With death across the heavenly seas
    Of fiery Trafalgar—

Nor Arthur's Knights amid the gloom
    Their knightly deeds have starred,
Nor Gallic Henry's matchless plume,
    Nor peerless-born Bayard—

Not all that antique fables feign
    And Orient dreams disgorge;
Nor yet the silver cross of Spain
    And lion of St. George

Can bid thee pale! Proud emblem still
    Thy crimson glory shines
Beyond the lengthened shades that fill
    Their proudest kingly lines.

Sleep on, thine own historic might,
    And be thy blazoned scroll;
A warrior's banner takes its flight
    To greet the warrior's soul.

Who loves the State that gave him birth,
  Till her proud sovereignty be won.
What though with toil,
  What th
Huzza! h
  We re-e

Not
Sin
The
L
Thi
L
"No
But by their own conse

For this they fought as Saxons fight,
  On bloody fields and long—
Themselves the champions of the right
  And judges of the wrong;
For this their stainless knighthood wore
  The branded rebel's name,
Until the starry cross they bore
  Set all the skies aflame!

And States co-equal and distinct
  Outshone the Western sun,

By one great charter interlinked—
  Not blended into one;
Whose graven key that high decree
  The grand inscription lent,
" No earthly power can rule the free
  But by their own consent!"

Oh, sordid age! oh, ruthless rage!
  Oh, sacrilegious wrong!
A deed to blast the record-page,
  And snap the strings of song:
In that great charter's name, a band
  By grovelling greed enticed,
Whose warrant is the grasping hand
  Of creeds without a Christ!

States that have trampled every pledge
  Its crystal code contains,
Now give their swords a keener edge
  To harness it with chains—
To make a bond of brotherhood
  The sanction and the seal,
By which to arm a rabble brood
  With fratricidal steel.

Who, conscious that their cause is black,
  In puling prose and rhyme,
Talk hatefully of love and tack
  Hypocrisy to crime:
Who smile and sneak, then "heave the gorge"
  Or impotently frown:

And call us "rebels" with King George
As if they wore his crown!

Most venal of your venal race,
Who think you cheat the sky
With every pharisaic face
And simulated lie;
Round Freedom's lair, with weapons bare,
We greet the light divine
Of those who throned the goddess there,
And yet inspire the shrine!

Our loved ones' graves are at our feet,
Their homesteads at our back—
No belted Southron can retreat
With women on his track:
Peal, bannered host, the proud decree
Which from your fathers went,
"No earthly power can rule the free
But by their own consent."

RE-ENLISTED FOR THE WAR.

BY MURRAY WALTON CRAIG—(M. W. CHAPMAN).

They bid us quit the hopeless strife,
They bid us lay our weapons by,
And they'll in mercy spare our life,
Although we're traitors doom'd to die;
But hark the sound that comes from far,
"Re-enlisted for the war."

And do the idiots dream that we
  Will e'er our holy cause desert,
Or cease our struggle to be free,
  And ev'ry freeman's right assert?
    Then hark the watchword from afar,
    " Re-enlisted for the war."

From ev'ry camp-fire in the land,
  From Florida to Tennessee;
From Texas to the fleeting sand
  Wash'd by the broad Atlantic sea,
    Oh, hark the watchword near and far,
    " Re-enlisted for the war."

All glory to that gallant band
  Of noble privates in the ranks!
In arms the patriot phalanx stand,
  And well deserve a nation's thanks;
    Their watchword comes from near and far,
    " Re-enlisted for the war."

And let the silent tear-drop fall
  For those who die upon the field;
No more they answer duty's call;
  With martyr blood their faith they've seal'd;
    Their dying watchword sounds afar,
    " Re-enlisted for the war."

Full many a mother mourns a son,
  Full many a wife is widow'd now;
Of many a lost beloved one,

Remorseless death has paled the brow;
  But still the watchword comes from far,
  "Re-enlisted for the war."

Were ever people yet subdued
  Who knelt at such a sacred shrine,
With souls so thoroughly imbued
  With freedom's principle divine?
    Whose watchword sounded from afar,
    "Re-enlisted for the war?"

Were ever people conquered yet
  Whose trust in God has never swerv'd?
Whose soil with freemen's blood is wet?
Whose hearts unflinching courage nerv'd?
    Whose watchword sounded near and far,
    "Re-enlisted for the war?"

MY SOLDIER BOY.

BY L. E. GRAYSON.

I am dreaming, ever dreaming of a silver-sanded shore,
Where the blue waves softly murmur as they roll forever more,
Where the sunbeams, brightly glowing, kiss the wavelets as they flow,
And the scented breeze is sighing where the orange flowers blow,
Till the music of its waters, with their cadence low, I hear,
As it mingles with the sighing breeze, and falls upon my ear,
And I seem to breathe the odors that are wafted from that shore,
Where my heart is fondly turning, fondly turning evermore.

When the sunset melts in glory, and the daylight softly dies,
Till the purple twilight deepens, and o'er all the splendor flies

Where no voice nor sound is heard, save the whisperings of the breeze,
As evening chants her vespers low among the leafy trees,
As I watch the golden hues that fade and vanish from my sight,
Like the hopes and dreams of lighter years, when lost in gloomy night,
More glorious is the sunset fairy pictures of that shore,
Where my heart is fondly turning, fondly turning evermore.

Do you ask why I am dreaming ever dreaming of that shore?
Why the music of its waters seems to haunt me evermore?
There encamp'd are Southern hearts close to that murmuring sea,
And a soldier boy among them, who's is one is dear to me,
Who, with that gallant hero-band, in his country's hour of need,
When danger threaten'd, at her call, resolved to save or bleed;
And there, ba like to the murmur sea, their white tents dot the shore,
Where my heart is fondly turning, fondly turning evermore.

When the tranquil earth is dreaming in the soft cool race of night,
And the quiet stars are keeping holy watch upon each height,
When angel eyes of saints seem their gentle watch to keep,
While some are wrapp'd in slumbers light, and some are left to weep,
When by that camption I saunces the solemn midnight round,
And my soldier boy is keeping watch, or slumbering on the ground,
I am praying heaven to guard from ill that silver-sanded shore,
Where my heart is fondly turning, fondly turning evermore.

THE LIFTING OF THE BANNER.

BY A. B. MEEK.

Lift aloft our glorious banner,
   Radiant with the Cross we love!
Over mountain, vale, savanna,
   Planet-gemmed, it floats above!
Through the storm and smoke of battle,
   Like an angel's wing, it waves.

Where the thunderous death-bolts rattle,
And the fiend of carnage raves!

Lift aloft that trophied glory,
Let it fondle with the breeze;
It shall live in deathless story,
It shall gleam on foaming seas.
Never, when our eyes behold it,
Shall our hearts feel doubt or fear;
Should we fall, oh! comrades, told it
Proudly round the soldier's bier!

Thrice it shone on grim Manassas,
Like a meteor from afar;
Through Virginia's mountain passes,
It was aye our guiding star;
Sharpsburg's blood-shot eyes beheld it,—
Richmond, with her Seven Days;
Chickamauga's breezes swelled it,—
Charleston still its fold displays.

Lighting up the Indian ocean,
Flashing on Atlantic seas,—
Now amid the Gulf's commotion,
Now before Pacific's breeze,
Dauntless champions proudly bear it,
Striking terror where they go;
All the Northern navies fear it;
Symbol of defeat and woe!

Lift it up, then, hallowed standard,
Scorched by fire and stained by blood!

It shall lead fair freeedom's vanguard,
  On the field and o'er the flood;
Here we vow by Heaven above us,
  By our mothers, sisters, wives,
By all tender hearts that love us,
  We'll protect it with our lives!

THE UNIFORM OF GREY.

BY EVA \ ELBERT.

The Briton boasts his coat of red,
  With lace and spangles decked;
In garb of green, the French are seen,
  With gaudy colors flecked;
The Yankees strut in dingy blue,
  And epauletts display;
Our Southern girls more proudly view
  The uniform of grey.

That dress is worn by gallant hearts
  Who every foe defy,
Who stalwart stand, with battle brand,
  To conquer or to die!
They fight for freedom, hope and home,
  And honor's voice obey,
And proudly wear where'er they roam
  The uniform of grey.

What though 'tis stained with crimson hues,
  And dim with dust and smoke,

By bullets torn, and rent and shorn
By many a hostile stroke;
The march, the camp, the bivouac,
The onset and the fray
But only serve more dear to make
The uniform of grey.

When wild war's tiger-strife is past,
And liberty restored;
When independence reigns at last,
By valor's arm secured;—
The South will stand, erect and grand,
And loftiest honors pay
To those who bore her flag, and wore
The uniform of grey.

And woman's love, man's best reward,
Shall cluster round their path,
And soothe and cheer the volunteer
Who dared the foeman's wrath.
Bright wreaths she'll bring and roses fling
Around his triumph-way,
And long in song thy fame prolong,
Old uniform of grey.

Lorena.

This was the great sentimental song of the war period.

The years creep slowly by, Lorena;
 The snow is on the grass again;
The sun's low down the sky, Lorena;
 The frost gleams where the flowers have been.
But the heart throbs on as warmly now
 As when the summer days were nigh;
Oh, the sun can never dip so low
 Adown affection's cloudless sky.

A hundred months have passed, Lorena,
 Since last I held that hand in mine,
And felt the pulse beat fast, Lorena,
 Though mine beat faster far than thine.
A hundred months—'twas flowery May,
 When up the hilly slope we climbed,
To watch the dying of the day
 And hear the distant church bells chimed.

We loved each other then, Lorena,
 More than we ever dared to tell;
And what we might have been, Lorena,
 Had but our loving prospered well!
But then, 'tis past, the years have gone,
 I'll not call up their shadowy forms;
I'll say to them, Lost years, sleep on,
 Sleep on, nor heed life's pelting storms.

The story of the past, Lorena,
 Alas! I care not to repeat;
The hopes that could not last, Lorena,
 They lived, but only lived to cheat.
I would not cause e'en one regret
 To rankle in your bosom now—
"For if we try we may forget,"
 Were words of thine long years ago.

Yes, these were words of thine, Lorena—
 They are within my memory yet—
They touched some tender chords, Lorena,
 Which thrill and tremble with regret.
'Twas not thy woman's heart which spoke—
 Thy heart was always true to me;
A duty stern and piercing broke
 The tie which linked my soul with thee.

It matters little now, Lorena,
 The past is in the eternal past;
Our hearts will soon lie low, Lorena,
 Life's tide is ebbing out so fast.
There is a future, oh, thank God!
 Of life this is so small a part—
'Tis dust to dust beneath the sod,
 But there, up there, 'tis heart to heart.

panied by a card or paper having the same *non de plume* written upon it, and containing the ful[l] name and address of the sender.

The fifty ($50) dollars will be awarded as f[ol]lows:

$20 to the writer of the best story.
15 "   "   "   "   " 2d best story.
10 "   "   "   "   " 3d "   "
5 "   "   "   "   " 4th "   "

WAR JOURNAL PUBLISHING COMPANY
[i]es and partisan publications, has been pres[ented to]
[to] the world. The Southern view has been [ex]ploited, although Mr. Davis, Mr. Ste[phens]

ANNIE OF THE VALE.

NEW WORDS—BY PAUL PILLEY.

The full moon is glowing,
 Her silver light throwing
O'er orchard and meadow, garden and grove.
 Her sweet rays are dancing,
 On clear waters glancing,
Along whose willowy margin I rove.
 Then come, come, love, come,
 Come, ere the lustre shall fail;
 Come in thy splendor, so graceful and tender,
 Dear Annie, sweet Annie of the Vale.

 The night-flower blooming,
 The breeze is perfuming,
While dew-drops glisten on leaflet and limb;
 And, far through the bowers,
 In these witching hours,
Ghost-like, is heard the Whip-poor-will's hymn
 Then come, come, love, come,
 Come ere the sweetness shall fail;
 Come in thy splendor, so graceful and tender,
 Dear Annie, sweet Annie of the Vale.

 I stand 'neath thy lattice,
 Where rose and clematis,
Like fond lovers' arms, around it entwine;
 Oh, would I could clasp,
 In my heart-throbbing grasp,

That beautiful form, so pure and divine.
Then come, come, love, come,
Come ere the witchery fail;
Come in thy splendor, so graceful and tender,
Dear Annie, sweet Annie of the Vale.

Thy soldier-bard straying,
His lute now is playing,
Thy heart to soothe with love's passionate spell;
He leaves thee the morrow,
And, lone in his sorrow,
Would breathe in thine ear his fondest farewell.
Then come, come, love, come,
Come ere these echoes shall fail;
Come in thy splendor, so graceful and tender,
Dear Annie, sweet Annie of the Vale.

THE APPROACH OF BATTLE.

Air— "*Ye banks and braes.*"

Along the hills and valleys low,
  With arms that turn the slanting ray,
See the proud legions of the foe,
  Sign of another bloody day!
With spangled banners flaunting high,
  With horse, and foot, and music grand,
With all yon pomp and pageantry,
  They've come to rule our sunny land.
Oh, Southern men, remember now
  The cause in which we stand arrayed!

Will you beneath their sceptre bow?
  See those you love, their vassals made?
Remember wrongs already done,
  Our women scourged, homes wrapped in flame,
And swear that yonder rising sun
  Shall set upon their flight and shame!

Be mindful of the glorious days,
  When Stonewall Jackson planned and led,—
We'll fight beneath his spirit's gaze,
  'Neath that of all our hallowed dead.
Hark, 'tis the cannon's opening roar!
  Now this the prayer we raise on high:
That we, before this day is o'er,
  May conquer, or like heroes, die!

LAMENT FOR MUMFORD.

Inscribed to his Wife and Children.

BY MISS J. M. PORTER.

Air—"*Long Weary Day.*"

Where murdered Mumford lies
  Bewailed in bitter sighs,
Low bowed beneath the flag he loved,
  Martyrs of Liberty,
  Defenders of the free!
    Come humbly nigh
    And learn to die!

Ah! Freedom on that day
  Turned fearfully away,
And pitying angels lingered near
  To gaze upon the sod
Stained with a hero's blood!
  While on his bier
Fell woman's tear!

Oh God! that he should die
  Beneath a Southern sky
Upon a felon's gallows swung!
  Murdered by a tyrant's band,
While round a helpless band
  On Butler's name
Breathed foulest shame!

But hark! loud peans fly
  From earth to vaulted sky!
He's crowned at Freedom's holy throne!
  List! sweet voiced Israfel
Tolls for the martyr's knell!
  Shout Southrons high
Our battle cry!

Lo at our hero's bourne
  Where Southern women mourn!
Come, valiant sons, bow at His shrine;
  Here, while devout we kneel,
Despots our hate shall feel!
  For Liberty
How sweet to die!

Come ye of Southern blood,
  Come kneel to Freedom's God!
Here, at her altars, vengeance swear;
  As cursed forever more,
Spurn the vile flag he tore!
  O'er Mumford's grave
Our banner wave!

*Israfel is this — we dost v[...] m n[...] w[...] chants around God's throne.—*German Legend.*

FAREWELL.

BY R. B. TRIMMIER.

Oh! Mary, love, farewell!
  I go to death and danger;
I go to meet in conflict fell
  The proud invading stranger.

I leave thee, love, to save
  The land we dearly cherish,
To break the yoke that binds the brave,
  To rescue or to perish.

Oh! Mary, love, thy light
  No more shall shine before me,
The flame of war grows redly bright,
  Destruction hovers o'er me.

But weep not, love, for me;
  Remember, though we sever,
The patriot who falls will be
  With glory crowned forever!

FORREST'S BATTLE CHORUS.

Respectfully dedicated to Major General N. B. Forrest.

BY REUBEN NASON.

On! our flag waves gladly o'er us,
  Flashing swords our way shall clear;
God's with us, our cause victorious,
Foemen dread th' avengers near.
  On! our flag waves gladly o'er us,
    Flashing swords our way shall clear;
  God's with us, our cause victorious,
    Foemen dread th' avengers near.

Comrades on! the field of glory
Woos us now with promise high;
Ours a place in deathless story;
  Comrades on! to do or die.
    On! our flag waves gladly o'er us,
      Flashing swords our way shall clear;
    God's with us, our cause victorious,
      Foemen dread th' avengers near

Brothers on! our land is wasted
By a hireling ruffian throng;
On! ere those we love have tasted
Insult, death or nameless wrong.
  On! our flag waves gladly o'er us,
    Flashing swords our way shall clear;
  God's with us, the foe before us,
    Let them dread th' avengers near.

Southrons on! no stain e'er rested
On our proud, chivalric name—
Scoff o' yonder race detested—
 On! for vengeance, home and fame!
  On! our flag waves gladly o'er us,
  Flashing swords, our way shall clear;
 God's with us, they quail before us—
  Strike! for all we hold most dear.

ASHBY.

BY JOHN R. THOMPSON.

To the brave all homage render:
 Weep, ye skies of June;
With a radiance pure and tender,
 Shine, oh sadden'd moon;
Dead upon the field of glory,
 Hero fit for song and story,
Lies our bold dragoon.

Well they learn'd, whose hands have slain him,
 Braver, knightlier foe
Never fought with Moor or Paynim,
 Rode at Templestowe;—
With a mien how high and joyous
 'Gainst the hordes that would destroy us
Went he forth, we know.

Nevermore, alas! shall sabre
  Gleam around his crest:
Fought his fight, fulfill'd his labor,
  Still'd his manly breast,
All unheard sweet nature's cadence,
  Trump of fame and voice of maidens,
Now he takes his rest.

Earth, that all too soon hath bound him,
  Gently wrap his clay;
Linger lovingly around him,
  Light of dying day;
Softly fall ye, summer showers;
  Birds and bees among the flowers,
Make the gloom seem gay.

There, throughout the coming ages,
  When his sword is rust,
With his deeds in classic pages.
  Mindful of her trust,
Shall Virginia, bending lowly,
  Still a ceaseless vigil holy
Keep above his dust.

The Southern Maiden to her Valentine.

BY MARGARITA J. CANEDO.

Air— *My lone rock by the sea.*

I give to thee, my soldier dear,
  My bosom's love and faith—
A faith that shall not falter, till
  This heart be cold in death;
I do not, with them, offer now
  The hand I keep for thee;
No marriage bells must ring for us
  Till our dear land is free.

Go forth into the field, beloved!
  My love thy shield shall be,
While in the home thy valor guards
  I watch and wait for thee.
Strike at thy country's hated foe!—
  I'll be a hero's bride;
Or if in death thou liest low,
  I'll mourn for thee with pride.

Now, now, while freedom's trumpets blow,
  While freedom's banners wave,
And call on all to meet the foe,
  Shrink not thou, Southern brave!
Home, Hope and Honor bid thee forth,—
  Fame's heralds wait on thee;
The maid thou lov'st for thee shall twine
  The wreath of victory.

Shall any, shrinking from the war,
    Fly trembling and afraid?
Let not that wretched coward dare
    Address a Southern maid;
Our hearts are only for the brave,
    Our hands are for the free;
March on where glory's banners wave,
    March on to victory!

"TRY US!"
Song of the Quitman Fencibles.
BY FRANCIS BAKER, DECEASED.

Our maiden banner courts the wind:
    Its stars are beaming o'er us;
Each radiant fold, now unconfined,
    Is floating free before us.
It bears a motto proud and high,
    For those who dare defy us;
And loud shall be our slogan-cry,
    Whene'r they come to "Try Us."

The hallowed ray that freedom gave,
    To cheer the gloom that bound us,
And shone in beauty o'er the brave,
    Still brightly beams around us.
The day our fathers bravely won
    Shall long be greeted by us;
And loudly through our ranks shall run
    The gallant war-cry, "Try Us."

Now fill the wine-cup to the brim,
  Fill, fill the ruby treasure;
Pour one libation forth to Him,
  Nor stint the burning measure.
And o'er the board, or in the field,
  His spirit shall be nigh us;
The patriot's hope, the soldier's shield,
  Whene'er they come to "Try Us."

Then give our banner to the wind,
  It's stars are beaming o'er us,
Its maiden folds now unconfined
  Are floating free before us;
It bears a motto proud and high,
  For those who dare defy us;
And loud shall be our slogan-cry,
  Whene'er they come to "Try Us."

OUR COUNTRY'S ENSIGN.

BY THE AUTHOR OF "SOUTHLAND," THE PRIZE SONG.

Air — "*Sparkling and bright.*"

Spotless and fair, in morning air
  Our lilly-hued flag is streaming;
And on it spread, in blue and red,
  The starry gemmed Cross is beaming!
    Then gladly greet that standard-sheet
      With music's swelling chorus;
    No spirit can fail, nor timidly quail,
      With that bright symbol o'er us!

Floating aloft, in battle oft
We have seen it proudly waving,
While round it fell, bomb, ball and shell,
Where Havoc's red fiends were raving!
    Then gladly greet that standard-sheet
    With music's swelling chorus;
    No spirit can fail, nor timidly quail,
    With that bright symbol o'er us!

Foemen shall fly when it on high
Exhibits it stainless splendors,
They cannot stand the lightning brand
Of Liberty's brave defenders!
    Then gladly greet that standard sheet
    With music's swelling chorus;
    No spirit can fail nor timidly quail,
    With that bright symbol o'er us!

Banner of white, so pure and bright,
By beauty's fair fingers woven,
Her starry eyes begem thy dyes,
And oft thy prowess have proven!
    Then gladly greet that standard-sheet
    With music's swelling chorus;
    No spirit can fail nor timidly quail
    With that bright symbol o'er us!

Stream on! stream on! child of the sun!—
Chaste emblem of national glory!—

Thy field so white shall soon glow bright
With triumph's immortal story!
Then gladly greet that standard-sheet
With music's swelling chorus;
No spirit can fail nor timidly quail
With that bright symbol o'er us!

A CRY TO ARMS.

BY HENRY TIMROD.

Ho! woodsmen of the mountain side!
Ho! dwellers in the vales!
Ho! ye who by the chafing tide,
Have roughen'd in the gales!
Leave barn and byre, leave kin and cot,
Lay by the bloodless spade,
Let desk, and case, and counter rot,
And burn your books of trade!

The despot roves your fairest lands,
And till he flies or fears,
Your fields must grow but armed hands,
Your sheaves be sheayes of spears!
Give up to mildew and to rust
The useless tools of gain;
And feed your country's sacred dust
With floods of crimson rain!

Come with the weapons at your call,
With musket, pike or knife;

He wields the deadliest blade of all
  Who lightest holds his life.
The arm that drives its unbought blows
  With all a patriot's scorn,
Might brain a tyrant with a rose,
  Or stab him with a thorn!
Does any falter? let him turn
  To some brave maiden's eyes,
And catch the holy fires that burn
  In those sublunar skies.
Oh! could you like your women feel,
  And in their spirit march,
A day might see your lines of steel
  Beneath the victor's arch!

What hope, O God! would not grow warm
  When thoughts like these give cheer?
The lily calmly braves the storm,
  And shall the palm tree fear?
No! rather let its branches court
  The rack that sweeps the plain;
And from the lily's regal port
  Learn how to breast the strain.

Ho! woodsmen of the mountain's side!
  Ho! dwellers in the vales!
Ho! ye, who by the roaring tide
  Have roughened in the gales!
Come! flocking gaily to the fight,
  From forest, hill, and lake!
We battle for our country's right,
  And for the lily's sake!

THE LONE STAR FLAG.

BY H. L. FLASH.

Up with the Lone Star banner!
 Its hues are still as bright
As when its glories braved the breeze
 At San Jacinto's fight:
Its fluttering folds in triumph waved
 O'er many a gory brow:
The freedom that was conquered then,
 Will not be yielded now.

The honor of that Lone Star flag
 That floats the blue above,
Is held as dear by Texan hearts,
 As that of her they love;
And not a stain shall dim its hues,
 While yet a man remains
To save this flower-girdled land
 From ignominious chains.

That banner, with the single star,
 Is Freedom's favored sign;
Beneath its unpolluted folds
 Her purest glories shine;
And in the whirlwind and the storm,
 Amid the crash and jar,
Her brightest hope still rests upon
 That solitary star.

THE SEA-KINGS OF THE SOUTH.

BY E. C. B.

Full many have sung of the victories our warriors have won,
From Bethel by the eastern tide to sunny Galveston—
On fair Potomac's classic shore, by sweeping Tennessee,
Hill, rock and river, shall tell forever the vengeance of the free.

The air still rings with the cannon shot, with battle's breath is warm,
Still on the hills their swords have saved, our legions wheel and form,
And Johnston, Beauregard and Lee, 'mid all their gallant train,
Wait yet at their head, in silence dread, the hour to charge again.

But a ruggeder field than the mountain side, a broader field than the
 plain,
Is spread for the fight in the stormy wave and the globe-embracing
 main;
'Tis there the keel of the goodly ship must trace the fate of the land,
For the name ye write in the sea foam white, shall first and longest
 stand.

For centuries on centuries, since erst the hollow tree
Was launched by the lone mariner on some primeval sea,
No stouter stuff than the heart of oak, or light elastic pine,
Had ventured beyond the shallow shoal, to pass the burning Line.

The naiad and the dryad met in billow and in spar;
The forest fought at Salamis, the groves at Trafalgar;
Old Tubal Cain had sweated again to forge the brand and ball,
But failed to frame the mighty hull that hold enfortressed all.

Six thousand years had left it for our nobler tars to show,
That iron was to ride the waves and timber sink below;
The waters bland that welcomed first the white man to our shore,
Columbus of an iron world, the brave Buchanan, bore.

Not gun for gun, but forty to one, the odds he had to meet!
One craft untried of wind or tide to board the haughty fleet!

Above her honored relics now the billows break and pour,
But the glory of that wondrous day is hers for evermore!

See yonder speck on the mist so far, as dim as in a dream!
Anear it speeds. There are masts like reeds, and a tossing plume of
  steam;
Fleet, fierce and gaunt, with bows aslant, she dashes proudly on;—
Whence and whither, her prey to gather, the foe shall learn anon.

Oh! wide and green is her hunting park, and plentiful the game!
From the restless bay of old Biscay, to the Carib sea she came.
The catchers of the whale she caught; swift *Ariel* overhauled;
And made Hatteras know the hardest *blow* that ever a tar appalled.

She bears the name of a noble State, and sooth she bears it well.
To us she hath made it a word of pride—to the Northern ear a knell;
To the Puritan in his busy mart, the Puritan on his deck,
With *Alabama*, visions start of ruin, woe and wreck.

In vain his lubberly squadrons round her magic pathway swoop,
Admiral, Captain, Commodore, in gunboat, frigate, sloop!
Save to snatch a prize or a foe chastise, as their feeble art she foils,
She scorns a point from her course to veer, to baffle all their toils.

And bravely hath her sister-ship begun her young career.
Already hath her gentle name become a name of fear;—
The name that breathes of the orange bloom, of soft lagoons that roll
Round the home of the Roman of the West—the unconquered Seminole.

Like the Albatross and the tropic-bird, forever on the wing.
For them nor night nor breaking morn may rest or shelter bring;
All drooping from the weary cruise, or shattered from the fight,
No dear home-haven opes to them its arms with welcome bright.

Then side by side in our love and pride, be our men of the land and sea!
The fewer these, the sterner task, the greater their guerdon be!
The fairest wreath of amaranth, the fairest hands shall twine,
For the brows of our preux chevaliers, the Bayards of the brine.

The "stars and bars" of our sturdy tars, as gallantly shall wave,
As long shall live in the storied page, or the spirit-stirring stave,
As hath the Red Cross of St. George, or the Raven flag of Thor,
Or the flag of the sea, whate'er it be, that ever unfurled to war.

Then flout full high to their parent sky, those circled stars of ours!
Where'er the dark-hulled foeman floats, where'er his emblem towers;
Speak for the right, for the truth and light, through the gun's
  unmuzzled mouth,
And the fame of the Dane revive again, ye Vikings of the South

LAND OF MY FATHERS.

BY A. B. MEEK.

Fair land of my fathers!
   Bright clime of the sun!—
Whose mountains and meadows
   By valor were won,
   In the days long ago,
   When the tyranous foe
Came over the waters his prowess to show,—
   Thy sons will maintain
   What their ancestors gave,
   Or sleep every one
   In a patriot's grave!

Fair land of the Southron,
   By Washington won,
By Pinckney, and Sumter,
   And stout Marion;
   Baptized with their blood,
   In battle's red flood,

When tyrants around them in grim phalanx stood;
 Thou still must be free,
 Free from centre to shore.
 Or life's purple current
 For thee we will pour!

What though the dark despots,—
 The scum of the North,—
Now press round thy borders,
 Now tread on thine earth,—
 We'll rise in full might,
 For the field and the fight,
And strike for wives, children, God, freedom and
 Neath the flag of the Cross, [right!
 With its stars all aglow,
 We'll swoop on the ranks
 Of the infidel foe!

Sure He, who the nations
 In justice doth sway,
Will guard us and guide us
 In battle's dread day.
 His children He led
 When from Egypt they fled,
And left in the Red Sea their enemies dead!
 A new Pharaoh now
 Seeks to vanquish this land,—
 Oh God! hurl him down
 With thy thunder-nerved hand!

Yes, land of my fathers!
　　　Dear home of my hope!
Bright land of the future!—
　　　Thou yet shall stand up
　　　Triumphant and strong,
　　　In battle and song,
The victor and queen of the jubilant throng!
　　　Far down through the years
　　　I see thy states rise,
　　　Independent and free,
　　　With their domes in the skies!

THE SOLDIER'S HEART.

BY F. P. BEAUFORT.

The trumpet calls, and I must go
To meet the vile invading foe;
But listen, dearest, ere we part—
Thou hast, thou hast the soldier's heart!

It could not be so true to thee
Were it not true to Liberty;
Far rather fill a soldier's grave
Than live a dastard and a slave!

Thine eyes shall light dark danger's path,
The gloomy camp, the foeman's wrath;
Above the battle's fiery storm,
I shall behold thy beauteous form!

With thoughts of thee for thy dear sake,
Redoubled efforts I will make;
And strike with an avenging hand
For lady-love and native land!

Then fare thee well, the trumpet's sound
Commands me to the battle-ground;
But listen, dearest, ere we part—
Thou hast, thou hast the soldier's heart!

MY WIFE AND CHILD.

BY GEN. HENRY R. JACKSON, OF GEORGIA.

The tattoo beats, the lights are gone,
　The camp around in slumber lies;
The night with solemn pace moves on,
　And sad, uneasy thoughts arise.
I think of thee, oh, dearest one!
　Whose love my early life hath blest;
Of thee and him, our baby son,
　Who slumbers on thy gentle breast.

God of the tender, hover near
　To her whose watchful eye is wet;
The mother, wife—the doubly dear—
　And cheer her drooping spirits yet.
Now, while she kneels before Thy throne,
　Oh, teach her, Ruler of the Skies!
No tear is wept to Thee unknown,
　No hair is lost, no sparrow dies:

That thou canst stay the ruthless hand
 Of dark disease, and soothe its pain;
That only by Thy stern command
 The battle's lost, the soldier's slain.
By day, by night—in joy or woe—
 By fears oppressed, or hopes beguiled,
From every danger, every foe,
 Oh, God! protect my wife and child!

STONEWALL JACKSON'S WAY.

Come, stack arms, men! pile on the rails,
 Stir up the camp fire bright.
No matter if the canteen fails,
 We'll make a roaring night!
Here Shenandoah brawls along,
There burly Blue Ridge echoes strong,
To swell the brigade's rousing song
 Of "Stonewall Jackson's Way."

We see him now—the old slouched hat
 Cocked o'er his eyes askew;
The shrewd dry smile—the speech so pat—
 So calm, so blunt, so true.
The "Blue-Light Elder" knows 'em well;
Says he, "That's Banks—he's fond of shell.
Lord save his soul!—we'll give him"—well;
 That's "Stonewall Jackson's way."

Silence! ground arms! kneel all! caps off!
 Old Blue-Light's going to pray.

Strangle the fool that dare's to scoff!
  Attention! it's his way:
Appealing from his native sod,
  In *forma pauperis*, to God—
" Lay bare thine arm—stretch forth thine rod:
  Amen!" That's "Stonewall's way!"

He's in the saddle now! Fall in!
  Steady! the whole brigade!
Hill's at the ford, cut off: we'll win
  His way out, ball and blade.
What matter if our shoes are worn?
What matter if our feet are torn?
"Quick step! we're with him ere the morn!"
  That's "Stonewall Jackson's way."

The sun's bright lances rout the mists
  Of morning—and, by George!
Here's Longstreet, struggling in the lists,
  Hemmed in an ugly gorge.
Pope and his Yankees, whipped before;
" Bay'nets and grape!" hear Stonewall roar:
"Charge, Stuart!—pay off Ashby's score!"
  Is "Stonewall Jackson's way."

Ah! maiden, wait and watch, and yearn
  For news of Stonewall's band.
Ah! widow, read with eyes that burn
  That ring upon thy hand!

Ah! wife, sew on, pray on, hope on:
Thy life shall not be all forlorn.
The foe had better ne'er been born
That gets in Stonewall's way!"

THE DRUMMER-BOY OF SHILOH.

On Shiloh's dark and bloody ground
   The dead and wounded lay;
Amongst them was a drummer-boy,
   Who beat the drum that day.
A wounded soldier held him up,
   His drum was by his side,
He clasped his hands, then raised his eyes,
   And prayed before he died.

"Oh, Mother!" said the dying boy,
   "Look down from Heaven on me,
Receive me to thy fond embrace,
   Oh, take me home to thee.
I've loved my country and my God,
   To serve them both I've tried."
He smiled, shook hands, Death seized the boy,
   Who prayed before he died.

Each soldier wept then like a child—
   Stout hearts were they, and brave;
The flag his winding-sheet, God's Book
   The key unto his grave.
They wrote upon a single board
   These words: "This is a guide

To those who'd mourn the Drummer-Boy,"
Who prayed before he died.

Ye angels round the throne of grace,
Look down upon the braves
Who fought and died on Shiloh's plain,
Now slumbering in their graves.
How many homes made desolate,
How many hearts have sighed,
How many like that Drummer-Boy,
Who prayed before he died!

MY LOVE AND I.

BY ASA HARTZ.

My love reposes on a rosewood frame—
　　A bunk have I;
A couch of feathery down fills up the same—
　　Mine's straw, but dry;
She sinks to sleep at night with scarce a sigh—
With waking eyes I watch the hours creep by.

My love her daily dinner takes in state—
　　And so do I (?);
The richest viands flank her silver plate—
　　Coarse grub have I;
Pure wines she sips at ease, her thirst to slake—
I pump my drink from Erie's limpid lake!

My love has all the world at will to roam—
　　Three acres I;

She goes abroad or quiet sits at home—
    So cannot I;
Bright angels watch around her couch at night—
A Yank, with loaded gun, keeps me in sight.

A thousand weary miles now stretch between
    My love and I;
To her, this wintry night, cold, calm, serene,
    I waft a sigh;
And hope, with all my earnestness of soul,
To-morrow's mail may bring my parole!

There's hope ahead! We'll one day meet again,
    My love and I;
We'll wipe away all tears of sorrow then.
    Her lovelit eye,
Will all my many troubles then beguile,
And keep this wayward reb. from Johnston's Isle.

THE WAR-CHILD.*

BY ANDERSON.

Awake! 'tis the call of the bugle, awake!
  Ho, Sergeant! go see to your steed—
Ere the morning light in the East shall break
  There'll be many a gallant deed!
Mount! mount! and away on the toilsome march!
  Our spirits are gay and light—

*General Wheeler.

Hurrah! hurrah! there is sport ahead,
  For the War-child rides to-night!

Thro' the aisles of the forest dark and grand,
  Where the meadows are ever gay;
Thro' the tangled paths of the wild woodland
  We will wind on our silent way,
And long ere the earliest stars go down,
  We will light us a glorious lamp,
And will laugh as the hated foe shall wake
  In the flames of his burning camp!

Ah! the devil will chuckle with joy full soon,
  For there's blood in the War-child's eye,
And death will ride out in the dark of the moon
  To where the foe slumbering lie,
And to-morrow a shadow will be on their land,
  And their people will wildly rave
For the sleepers whose sleep will be broken to-night
  By the clutch of the hungry grave!

In the front of the fight, in the face of the foe,
  At the rear midst battle's thunder—
'Tis there that the flash of our swords is seen
  As we rend their ranks asunder!
'Tis there that our little chief maketh his home,
  And the enemy ever hath found us—
'Tis there where the vault of the sky is our roof
  And our couches the heather around us!

Then hurrah for our chief! hurrah for our cause!
  Hurrah! for our glorious banner!

E

It shall float ere the blossoming of the leaf
 O'er each vale of our land and savannah!
Hurrah! for the spoils which our coming await!
 For the next who is fated to fall!
Hurrah! boots and saddles! at last we are off!
 Mount! mount! 'tis the bugler's call.

MY MARYLAND.

BY JAMES R. RANDALL.

The despot's heel is on thy shore,
 Maryland!
His torch is at thy temple door,
 Maryland!
Avenge the patriotic gore
That swept o'er gallant Baltimore,
And be the battle-queen of yore,
 Maryland! My Maryland!

Hark! to a wand'ring son's appeal,
 Maryland!
My Mother-State, to thee I kneel,
 Maryland!
For life and death, for woe and weal,
Thy peerless chivalry reveal,
And gird thy beauteous limbs with steel,
 Maryland! My Maryland!

Thou wilt not cower in the dust,
 Maryland!

Thy beaming sword shall never rust,
                Maryland!
Remember Carroll's sacred trust,
Remember Howard's war-like thrust.
And all thy slumberers with the just,
           Maryland! My Maryland!

Come! 'tis the red dawn of the day,
                Maryland!
Come with thy panoplied array,
                Maryland!
With Ringgold's spirit for the fray,
With Watson's blood at Monterey,
With fearless Lowe and dashing May,
           Maryland! My Maryland!

Dear Mother, burst the tyrant's chain,
                Maryland!
Virginia should not call in vain,
                Maryland!
She meets her sisters on the plain;
"*Sic Semper*," 'tis the proud refrain
That baffles minions back again,
                Maryland!
Arise in majesty again,
           Maryland! My Maryland!

Come! for thy shield is bright and strong,
                Maryland!
Come! for thy dalliance does thee wrong,
                Maryland!

Come to thine own heroic throng,
That stalks with liberty along,
And gave a new Key to thy song,
      Maryland! My Maryland!

I see the blush upon thy cheek,
      Maryland!
But thou wast ever bravely meek,
      Maryland!
But lo! there surges forth a shriek
From hill to hill, from creek to creek—
Potomac calls to Cheaspeake,
      Maryland! My Maryland!

Thou wilt not yield the Vandal toll,
      Maryland!
Thou wilt not crook to his control,
      Maryland!
Better the fire upon thee roll,
Better the shot, the blade, the bowl,
Than crucifixion of the soul,
      Maryland! My Maryland!

I hear the distant thunder-hum,
      Maryland!
The Old Line's bugle, fife and drum,
      Maryland!
She is not dead, nor deaf, nor dumb,
Huzza! she spurns the Northern scum!
She breathes—she burns! she'll come! she'll come!
      Maryland! My Maryland!

GEORGIA.

BY JAQUES JOURNOT.

Blessings on thee, Land of Beauty,
   Sleeping in a sunny clime!
Blessings on thy hills and valleys—
   I invoke them in my rhyme!
Far and wide my steps may wander,
   Fairer scenes may meet my eyes,
But my soul will cherish ever,
   Memories of thy glorious skies.

Northward, 'gainst the quiet heavens,
   Thy blue mountain barriers rise,
And above thy foaming torrents
   Glow the Iris' radiant dyes;
There *Tallulah* dashes madly
   Through the sundered granite hills,
And a sense of awful beauty
   All the gazer's being fills.

And *Tocooa*, haunt of fairies,
   And *Nacooche's* valley sweet,
Where the shining *Chattahoochee*
   Stars and sunshine love to greet;
And *Mount Yonah* soaring proudly,
   Where the winds are pure and free,
Wafts a greeting on their pinions,
   To his neighbor *Currahee*.

Thine the *Mountain Rock of Granite*,
  Rising 'mid thy fertile plains—
Nature's everlasting watchtower,
  Looking o'er thy wide domains;
Looking northward to the mountains—
  Southward o'er savannas wide,
Where through dark lagoons and marshes,
  Flows the *Altamaha's* tide.

Thine the lovely *Forest City*,
  Bonaventure's wealth of shade—
Classic *Athens*—seat of learning:
  And *Augusta's* mart of trade;
Macon shines, and fair *Columbus*,
  And, *Atlanta's* busy street,
And the pride of *Rome* the western,
  Where fair *Coosa's* waters meet.

But thy proudest treasures, Georgia.
  Are thy *Sons*, so brave and true—
And thy gentle, bright-eyed *Daughters*,
  Who with love our souls imbue;
Thine the valiant and the lovely—
  Manhood's strength and woman's charms—
And thy Homes adorned by Beauty,
  Guarded are by Valor's arms.

MISSOURI.

BY A. ALEXANDER.

Misouri! Missouri! bright Queen of the West!
Of all that is lovely in nature possessed;
Of flower-decked prairie, of river and rill,
Of broad fertile meadow, and forest-crowned hill;
Where hamlet and homestead, 'mid orchards of green,
And tall-steepled cities in splendor, are seen;—
How peerless thou wert, in the days long ago,
Ere trod o'er thy borders the feet of the foe!

Missouri! Missouri! my dear mother State,
How fallen thy fortunes, how sad is thy fate!
The storm-tide of battle sweeps over thy plains;
Thy fair limbs are fettered by tyranny's chains;
The sword and the faggot have blasted thy pride;
The blood of thy children thy soil has dyed;
The human hyenas now howl 'round thy shore,
And o'er thee the vultures insatiate roar!

Missouri! Missouri! how often in dreams,
The exile revisits thy beautiful streams!
The cottage he sees, where his forefathers dwelt!
The hearth, 'round whose circle his fair sisters knelt!
The grave where, by moonlight, he told his first love!
The graves of his kin, with the white stones above!
The spoiler is 'mid them,—great God! can it be,
Pollution like this is permitted by thee!

Missouri! Missouri! thou shalt be avenged!
The hearts of thy children cannot be estranged;
They've rushed to the field, and tho' driven afar,
They yet will return on the conqueror's car!
The blood of the Yankee and alien shall pay
For the havoc and shame of their infidel sway!
No prayers then for mercy our souls shall entice,
Our watchwords are Vengeance, Missouri, and Price!

THE STAR OF ALABAMA.

Written the day the Banner of Secession was erected on her Capitol.

BY A. B. MEEK.

The Star of Alabama floats proudly out to-day,
Upon yon field of azure, with independent ray.
The clouds that gloomed about it are rended from the sky,
And now in sovereign splendor it greets the patriot eye.

Oh, beamed it not as sweetly as Hesper in the West,
When Peace, with lillied fingers, wrapped roses round her breast?
But now, when grim Aggression is threatening ruthless wars,
It burns as fierce, defiant, as crimson tinted Mars.

The Polar Star of Freedom!—as sailors, o'er the sea,
Are guided through the midnight, so we are led by thee.
Shine on, with beams resplendent, thro' shadows and thro' storm,
No clouds can ever sully thy sky-emblazoned form.

The children of Chaldea, when gleamed the morning star,
Renewed their vows of homage before its golden car;
So we, beneath thy splendor, now lift our hands on high,
And swear to live as freemen, or freemen like to die!

Let carnage come, if need be ; let famine blight the land ;
Let pestilence and sorrow weigh down our patriot band;
Yet—God who rules the Nations !—we'd rather fill our graves,
Than live a race of cowards, a Northern tyrant's slaves !

Fair Star of Alabama!—not thine alone the pride,
A Sisterhood of Planets now clusters to thy side ;--
The Pleiades of Freedom !—lo ! how they flock above,
And flood the crystal valleys with symphonies of love !

Soon,—as in tropic regions, the Southern Cross is seen,
A constellated symbol, majestic and serene,—
Our war-won young Republics a galaxy shall form,
Which nations shall admire, nor despots dare to harm !

LOUISIANA.

Ho ! Louisiana !
  There is no clime like thine:
Land of the broad savanna,
  Land of the citron vine.
Land of the monarch river,
  Of lake and prairied plain,
Our free-born home forever,
  A beauteous, bright domain.

Above, the deep blue heaven
  Looks down with laughing eyes,
And breezes, mildly driven,
  Float o'er thy sunny skies.
Around, rich fields extending,
  Are clothed in emerald green,

And birds, their music blending,
  On every bough are seen.

With orange-blossoms laden;
  Or golden fruit, each bower
Reveals the dark-eyed maiden,—
  "Herself a fairer flower"—
The sunny Creole beauty,
  With voice of song and mirth,
And true to love and duty,
  The houries of the earth.

Ho! Louisiana!
  Home of the brave and free,
Thy fertile, broad savanna
  Goes smiling to the sea;
Where princely wealth inherits,
  And generous thoughts expand
The chivalric, high spirits,
  The guardians of the land.

I WOULD BE A SOLDIER STILL.

I have marched, and perils faced;
  On the blood-stained field I've slept:
In the midst of war's dread waste,
  O'er a comrade's grave, I've wept.

CHORUS—Might I march through life again,
  In spite of every by-gone ill,
To the end of life's campaign,
  I'd be a soldier still!

I've seen the pale-faced moon
  Shine o'er a hero's grave,
Where a gallant heart lay cold,
  Once noblest of the brave.
    Chorus—Might I march, etc.

I've seen the soldier fall,
  And heard his last sad sigh;
But my dearest wish is still
  For my country so to die.
    Chorus—Might I march, etc.

BATTLE CALL.

BY ARTHUR BELTON.

Come forth, ye gallant hearts, come forth!
  Who love this golden land,
And meet the fierce hordes of the North
  With pike and battle-brand!
Their crowding ships now stalk the deep,
  With wrath for us in store;
Oh come, and, with your strong arms, sweep
  The Vandals from our shore!

Come from each iron-girted hill—
  From every verdant grove;
Come from the fields your strong arms till—
  The homes your stout hearts love!

Oh, towns and cities, pour ye forth
    Your thousands for the fight!
And teach the vile, presumptuous North,
    Our land's resistless might!

Old man, dash down thy staff and crutch,
    And seize thy sword again;
Thy limbs shall feel youth's magic touch
    On Freedom's battle-plain.
And thou, oh lithe and fair-faced boy,
    Spring from thy mother's knee;
Her heart will thrill with patriot joy,
    Her soldier-son to see!

God goes with us to battle now;
    His storms have rent the foe:
Oh, let us kneel to Him and vow
    We will complete the blow!
By yonder consecrated cross—
    The standard of the sky—
We swear, whatever be the loss,
    To conquer or to die!

Then come, ye gallant hearts, come forth!
    Who love this golden land,
And meet the fierce hordes of the North
    Beside the ocean strand!
In vain their scowling squadrons loom
    Across the Mexic wave;
Hurl, hurl on them their rightful doom—
    Give them a felon's grave!

THE CAVALIERS OF DIXIE.

BY BENJ. F. PORTER.

Air—"Ye Mariners of England."

Ye Cavaliers of Dixie!
Who guard the Southern shores,
Whose standards brave the battle storm,
Which o'er the border roars;
Your glorious sabres draw once more,
And charge the Northern foe;
And reap their columns deep,
Where the raging tempests blow,
And the iron hail in floods descends,
And the bloody torrents flow.

Ye Cavaliers of Dixie!
Tho' dark the tempest lower,
What arms will wear the tyrant's chains,
What dastard heart will cower?
Bright o'er the night a sign shall rise
To lead to victory!
And your swords reap their hordes,
Where the battle tempests blow;
Where the iron hail in floods descends,
And the bloody torrents flow.

The South! she needs no ramparts,
No lofty towers to shield;
Your bosoms are her bulwarks strong,
Breastworks that never yield!
The thunders of your battle blades,

Shall sweep the servile foe;
While their gore stains the shore,
Where the battle tempests blow;
Where the iron hail in floods descends,
And bloody torrents flow.

The battle flag of Dixie!
With crimson field shall flame,
Her azure cross and silver stars,
Shall light her sons to fame!
When peace, with olive branch returns,
That flag's white folds s. .ll glow,
Still bright on every height,
When the storm has ceased to blow,
And the battle tempests roar no more,
Nor the bloody torrents flow.

Oh! battle flag of Dixie!
Long, long, triumphant wave!
Where'er the storms of battle roar.
Or victory crowns the brave!
The Cavaliers of Dixie!
In woman's song shall glow
The fame of your name,
When the storm has ceased to blow,
When the battle tempests rage no more,
Nor the bloody torrents flow.

ARM FOR THE SOUTHERN LAND.

BY GEN. MIRABEAU B. LAMAR.

Air—"*Oft in the Stilly Night.*"

Arm for the Southern Land;
　All fear of death disdaining;
Low lay the tyrant band,
　Our sacred rights profaning!
Each hero draws in freedom's cause,
　And meets the foe with bravery:
The servile race, and tory base,
　May safety seek in slavery.
Chains for the dastard knave—
　Recreant limbs should wear them;
But blessings on the brave
　Whose valor will not bear them!

Stand by your injured State,
　And let no feuds divide you;
On tyrants pour your hate,
　And common vengeance guide you.
Our foes should feel proud freemen's steel,
　For freemen's rights contending;
Where'er they die, there let them lie.
　To dust in scorn descending.
Thus may each traitor fall
　Who dare as foe invade us;
Eternal fame to all
　Who shall in battle aid us!

Proud land! shall she invoke
  Another's hand to right her?
No! her own avenging stroke
  Shall backward roll the smiter.
Ye tyrant band, with ropes of sand,
  Go bind the rushing river;
More weak and vain your cursed chain,
  While God is freedom's giver.
Then welcome to the day
  We meet the proud oppressor,
For God will be our stay,
  Our right-hand and redresser.

JEFFERSON DAVIS.

BY A. B. MEEK.

Air—"*The brave old oak.*"

A song for the Chief, the gallant Chief,
  Who hath rule in this Southern Land;
With heart and with mind, by Heaven designed
  To lead our patriot band.
On the crimson field, we have seen him wield
  The warrior's victor blade;
At the helm of State, more grand and more great,
  His wisdom he hath displayed.
    Then here's to the Chief, the lordly Chief,
      Our second Washington!—
    Thro' the trump of fame, great DAVIS' name
      Shall echo till time be done!

When her sons arose to confront the foes
Who sought to enslave the South,
And swore to maintain their rightful domain,
Despite the grim cannon's mouth;
They called from the West their bravest and best,
To guide thro' the gath'ring gloom;
And nobly and grand he's rescued the land
From tyranny's savage doom!
  Then here's to the Chief, &c.

We've others as great in Councils of State,
With voice as potent to save;
We've Knights in the field, whose deeds have revealed
A genius as skillful and brave;
But where can we find so aptly combined
The Soldier and Statesman as well,—
The Christian and Sage, the Pride of the Age,—
The Scholar, with classical spell?
  Then here's to the Chief, &c.

Long, long may he live, wise lessons to give,—
The hearts of the people to cheer;
A contrast how great to that Zany, whom Fate
Has throned in the Fed'ral sphere!
A Model of worth, a Star for the earth
To view with love and delight,—
A Pillar by day, to pilot the way,—
A Beacon for us at night!
  Then here's to the Chief, &c.

GOD SAVE THE SOUTH!

BY REUBEN NASON.

Air—"*God save the King.*"

God bless our Southern land!
Guard our beloved land!
    God save the South!
Make us victorious,
Happy and glorious,—
Spread Thy shield over us;—
    God save the South!

Oh, Lord of Hosts, arise!
Scatter our enemies,
    Who mock Thy truth:
Confound their politics,
Frustrate their knavish tricks,—
In Thee our faith we fix;—
    God save the South!

In the fierce battle hour,
With Thine Almighty Power,
    Assist our youth;—
May they, with victory crown'd,
Joining our choral round,
With heart and voice resound,
    "God save the South!"

HYMN TO THE DAWN.

BY A. J. REQUIER.

From an ominous rift in the pitiless sky
    That has darkened our desolate land,
Springs a luminous rill of auriferous dye,
    Gushing out of a mystical hand;
Upon valleys of carnage and mountains of fire—
    On the heaps of the holily slain—
It descends with the rush of a resonant lyre,
    And the gleam of a magical rain.

It unveils from the depths of its fountains of blue,
    Such a blaze of bewildering light
As the Legends of Araby never yet drew
    From the stars of traditional night;—
Purple acres of grape and savannahs of snow,
    Full of streams that enrichingly run
Thro' the fairest of blooms which the tropics bestow
    On the flowering Brides of the Sun.

Noble structures of Commerce and niches of Art,
    Stately temples and towers between,
Fretted domes, soaring up from the dust of the mart,
    Where the wonders of Science are seen;
Fluted pillars and urns to the primitive Past,
    And its young representative scions,
And bronzes heroic, colossally vast
    As the winged Assyrian Lions.

O, I see the long stretch of thy sorrowing years,
   Clime of azure! transformed in my sight,
From the comfortless drops of thine anguishing tears
   Into dews of maternal delight;
Royal anthems resounding on odorous seas—
   Sceptred barges that bridally toss,
With their white waving pennons unfurled to the breeze
   In the blush of a tremulous Cross!

Green idol of childhood! engirded by strife
   With a glory the grandest of Old,
Could they dream of the toils which encompass thy life,
   Would cry out from their cryptical mould:
God-anointed in War and exalted in Peace,
   I behold thee—abroad and at home—
With the beautiful lips of republican Greece,
   And the brow of imperial Rome.

THE GALLANT SOLDIER BOY.

BY PAUL PELBY.

Oh, the gallant soldier boy
   Is the lad whom I love dearly;
His beaming face, his smile of joy,
   His lip that speaks sincerely!
I met him in the willow grove,
   When for the combat he was starting;
We plighted then our faith and love,—
   Alas, the sorrow of that parting!

In his uniform of grey,
    He stood erect in martial beauty,
And sadly tore himself away,
    From arms of love, to claims of duty.
I twined my scarf around his neck,
    I placed my ring upon his finger,
I felt his kisses on my cheek,
    I wept, but could not bid him linger.

Oh, how slowly drags this war!
    Its weeks, and months, and years of sorrow!
My soldier boy still stays afar,—
    In vain I wait for each to-morrow.
The willow grove, with faded bowers,
    Seems for his tedious absence mourning;
Oh, watching stars, speed on the hours,
    When I shall greet his fond returning.

"SUMTER."

BY MISS E. C. SLOMAN.

Three cheers for gallant Sumter,
    Now bath'd in glory's ray;
To her we owe our safety,
    On this auspicious day.
A faithful sentinel she stands,
    To guard our Charleston port,
And all the annals of the past
    Record no braver fort;

Protected by God's rolling waves,
 No Monitors she'll dread,
And grand, defiant, tempest-toss'd,
 She nobly rears her head.

Her flag, now pierced by shot and shell,
 Still proudly holds its place,
Though every brick on Sumter's ground
 Is trembling to its base.
But stout hearts guard those crumbling walls;
 No breach can make them quail;
From every port-hole bursts the cry,
 "There's no such word as fail!"
And, phœnix-like, she'll rise again,
 A tower of strength to all,
For Carolina's sons have sworn
 Fort Sumter ne'er shall fall!

TENNESSEE.

BY S. NEWTON BERRYHILL.

Marching through the gloomy wildwood,
 Or in bivouac on the plain,
Thoughts of spots we loved in childhood
 Crowd upon the weary brain.
As a lost child's heart keeps yearning
 For its place on mother's knee,
So our thoughts are ever turning
 Back to dear old Tennessee.

CHORUS—Tennessee, dear Tennessee!
　　Whereso'er our lot may be,
　　Fondly turn our thoughts to thee—
　　Tennessee, sweet Tennessee!

On the crimson field of battle,
Wading through a sea of gore,
Loud above the muskets' rattle—
Loud above the cannons' roar,
We have heard her wails of anguish—
Shrieks for help when none are near—
Groans of fathers doomed to languish
In the prisons dark and drear.

And we've sworn—her hardy yeomen—
By the God who rules above,
That we'll drive the vandal foemen
From the dear old State we love;
From the altars where our fathers
Knelt in olden time to God,
And the graveyard where our mothers
Sleep beneath the hallowed sod.

We have sworn it! ye whose revels
Desecrate our childhood's home—
Sons of Moloch—bloody devils—
Tremble, for your hour has come.
Fierce-eyed Vengeance now is making
Bare his brawny, red right arm,
And the gleaming blade is shaking
That shall drink your life-blood warm.

We are coming! Fathers. Mothers,
Let the fainting hearts revive;
Fan the fire the tyrant smothers,
Keep the glowing spark alive.
Ere by Cumberland's blue waters
Fades the last wild rose of Spring,
Tennessee's own bright-eyed daughters
Shall our glorious triumph sing.

SONG OF VICTORY.

BY F. P. BEAUFORT.

Oh, peal the song of victory!
  A nation's joyous cry!
Our troops have met the enemy,
  And made his legions fly!
With musket, sword and bayonet,
  With rifle, spear and brand,
We met him in the deadly trench,
  And swept him from the land!

In vain his huge artillery
  From every hill-top played,
And through our lines of infantry,
  Long lanes of carnage made.
We fought for home and native land,
  For mothers, children, wives,
Nor heeded how our blood we spilt,
  Nor how we lost our lives.

We charged upon his batteries,
  We slew him where he stood,
Till all the lines and rivulets
  Ran red with human blood!
The shout, the curse, the scream, the groan,
  Rang through the smoky air,
While shrieking balls and bursting shells
  Fell hail-like on us there!

He met our onset gallantly,
  But when our gleaming steel
Flashed 'mid his sundered panoply,
  It made his columns reel!
They could not stand the lightning brand,
  The gory bayonet blade;
They turned and fled—all but the dead—
  Defeated and dismayed!

Ho, gallant men of Tennessee!
  Ho, Mississippi's sons!
Ho, Alabama's chivalry!
  And Georgia's fearless ones!
With Texan and Arkansan braves,
  And Louisiana's host,
Ye reaped the patriot's sweet revenge
  For all your land had lost!

Fair Florida's enamelled bowers
  Are flusht with fresher green;
And Carolinas' crowns of flowers
  On many a brow are seen!

Virginia to Kentucky shouts!
Missouri—Maryland!
All, all rejoice, with rapturous voice,
And greet their victor band!

TO THE RESCUE, ALABAMA!

BY A. B. MEEK.

To the rescue, Alabama!
  Land of fearless hearts and true!
Hark! the trumpet's martial clamor
Calls you now to War's wild drama—
  Bids your children UP AND DO!

Lo! the insolent invader,
  O'er your north line, pours his host;
And his grim and vast armada,
Like some lightning-winged tornado,
  Hovers 'round your southern coast!
          To the rescue, Alabama!

He is led by lust of plunder;
  He would cast your altars down;
All life's tenderest ties would sunder;
Blasting, as with bolts of thunder,
  Cottage, palace, farm and town!

Speed your clans from every valley,
  Pine-clad plain, and mountain high;
Let them not, like cravens, dally—

Bid them, 'neath you War-Cross, rally—
There to conquer or to die!
   To the rescue, Alabama!

Fling it forth—bright constellation!
Banner of the CRUCIFIED!
It shall prove our land's salvation—
Sign-baptismal of a nation!
 It shall quell the foeman's pride!

Let him come with ships and horses,
 Countless as the leaves and waves—
Vain are all his vast resources—
Conscience-smit, his venal forces
 Here shall meet defeat—and graves!
   To the rescue, Alabama!

Patrio's, when they stand united,
 Battling for their own loved land—
Heart to heart, heroic, plighted—
Never can be crushed or blighted
 By ten-fold their Spartan band!

Mother State, dear Alabama!
 Then to battle speed thy sons!
Bid *each* heed the trumpet's clamor—
Bid *all* act, in War's wild drama,
 Like so many Washingtons!
   To the rescue, Alabama!

THE VALIANT CONSCRIPT.

How are you, boys?—I'm just from camp,
  And feel as brave as Cæsar;
The sound of bugle, drum and fife,
  Has raised my Ebenezer.
I'm full of fight—odds, shot and shell!
  I'll leap into the saddle,
And when the Yankees see me come,
  Lord, how they will skedaddle!
    Hold up your head! up, Shanghai, Shanks!
      Don't shake your knees and blink so;
    It is no time now to dodge the act:
      Brave comrades, don't you think so.

I was a plough-boy in the field,
  A gawky, lazy dodger,
When came the Conscript officer,
  And took me for a sojer.
He put a musket in my hand,
  And showed me how to fire it:
I marched and countermarched all day:
  Lord, how I did admire it.
      Hold up your head! etc.

With corn and hog-fat for my food,
  And digging, guarding, drilling,
I got as thin as twice-skimmed milk,
  And was scarcely worth the killing;
But now I'm used to homely fare,
  My skin as tough as leather,

I do guard duty chearfully
  In every kind of weather.
      Hold up your head! etc.

I am brim full of fight, my boys;
  I would not give a thank ye
For all the smiles the girls can give,
  Until I've killed my Yankee!
High private is a glorious rank,
  There's wide room for promotion;
I'll get a corp'ral's stripe some day,
  When Fortune's in the notion.
      Hold up your head! etc.

'Tis true, I have not seen a fight,
  Nor have I smelt gunpowder;
But then, the way I'll pepper Yanks,
  Will be a sin to chowder.
A sergeant's stripes I soon will sport.
  Perhaps, be color-bearer,
And then a Captain—good for me!
  I'll be a regular tearer.
      Hold up your head! etc.

I'll then begin to wear the stars,
  And then the wreaths of glory,
Until an army I command,
  And poets sing my story.
Our Congress will pass votes of thanks
  To him who rose from zero:

The people in a mass will shout,
  "Hurrah! behold the hero!"
      Hold up your head! etc.

[*Fires his gun by accident.*]

What's that?—Oh, dear! a boiler's burst,
  A gas-pipe has exploded!
Maybe the Yankees are hard by,
  With muskets ready loaded.
On, gallant soldiers, beat them back!
  I'd join you in the frolic,
But I've a chill from head to foot,
  And symptoms of the colic!
      Hold up your head! etc.

THE POST OF DANGER.

BY GEN. MIRABEAU B. LAMAR.

Give to the poet his well-earned praise,
  And the songs of his love, preserve them;
Encircle his brows with fadeless bays,—
  The children of genius deserve them!
But never to me such praises breathe,—
  To the minstrel-feeling a stranger,—
I only sigh for the laurel wreath
  That a patriot wins in DANGER!

Speed, speed the day when to war I hie!
  The fame of the field is inviting;

Before my sword shall the foeman fly,
  Or fall in the flash of its lightning.
Away with song, and away with charms!
  Insulted Freedom's proud avenger,
I bear no love but the love of arms,
  And the bride that I woo is DANGER!

When shall I meet the audacious foe,
  Face to face, where the flags are flying?
I long to thin them "two at a blow,"
  And ride o'er the dead and the dying!
My sorrel steed shall his fetlocks stain
  In the brain of the hostile stranger;
With an iron heel he spurns the plain,
  And he breathes full and free in DANGER.

When victory brings the warrior rest,
  Rich the rewards of martial duty,—
The thanks of a land with freedom blest,
  And the smiles of its high-born beauty!
Does victory fail?—enough for me,
  That I fall not to fame a stranger;
His name shall roll with eternity
  Who finds the foremost grave in DANGER!

CLOCKNABEN.*

BY ARTHUR BELTON.

Brother-soldier, let us rally
   Round our country's lifted flag;
Who in such a cause can dally?
Who in such an hour can lag?
See approach the foul invaders,
   Trampling on our fathers' graves:
He would seize our wives and daughters;
   He would make our children slaves!

Long we bore, with tame submission,
   His aggressions on our rights,
While the hounds of Abolition
   Howled upon the Northern heights.
When at length they rent asunder
   All the bonds of love and faith,
Scorning to be slaves, we met them
   On the ensanguined field of death!

Let him come with all his legions;
   We will drive them beaten back.
Never shall these sunny regions

---

* This was the gathering cry of one of the clans of Scotland. Scott says, in the Antiquary: "They were stout hearts, the race of Glenatlan, male and female, and sae were a' that in auld times cried their gathering word of 'Clocknaben'—they stood shouther to shouther. Nae man parted from his chief for love of gold or of gain, or of right or of wrong."

Wilt beneath his Vandal track.
Sweep him from our dimpled valleys,
Crush him in the mountain pass:
Let no vestige, but his ashes,
Linger on the crimsoned grass!

Souls heroic—sons of sires
Who from despots won this land,
Feel ye not their patriot fires
Glowing yet in heart and hand!
Freedom's hallowed line of martyrs,
From their shining homes above,
Cry to us: "From vile pollution
Save our Legacy of Love!"

Now's the welcome dawn of battle!
Hark! the bugle's wailing sound!
Soon the bolts of death shall rattle—
Bomb and shell—these scenes around.
Brother-soldier, oh! then rally
Round our country's lifted flag;
Who in such a cause can dally?
Who in such an hour can lag?

THE SOUTHERN CROSS.

BY ST. GEORGE TUCKER.

Air—"The Star-Spangled Banner."

O! say, can you see through the gloom and the storm,
More bright for the darkness, that bright constellation?

Like the symbol of Love and Redemption its form,
  As it points to the haven of hope and the nation.
How radiant each star, as the beacon afar,
  Giving promise of peace, or assurance of war!
'Tis the Cross of the South, which shall ever remain
To light us to freedom and glory again!

How peaceful and blest was America's soil,
  Till betrayed by the guile of the Puritan demon,
Which lurks under virtue, and springs from its coil
  To fasten its fangs in the life-blood of freemen.
Then boldly appeal to each heart that can feel,
And crush the foul viper 'neath Liberty's heel;
And the Cross of the South shall in triumph remain
To light us to freedom and glory again!

'Tis the emblem of Peace, 'tis the day-star of Hope,
  Like the sacred "Labarum" that guided the Roman;
From the shores of the Gulf to the Delaware's slope,
  'Tis the trust of the Free and terror of foemen.
Fling its folds to the air, whilst we boldly declare
The rights we demand, or the deeds that we dare!
While the Cross of the South shall in triumph remain
To light us to freedom and glory again!

And if peace should be hopeless, and justice denied,
  And war's bloody vulture should flap its black pinions,
Then gladly "to arms!" while we hurl in our pride
  Defiance to tyrants and death to their minions!
With our front in the field, swearing never to yield,
Or return like the Spartan, in death on our shield!
And the Cross of the South shall triumphantly wave
As the Flag of the Free or the Pall of the Brave!

All Quiet Along the Potomac To-Night.

BY LAMAR FONTAINE.

"All quiet along the Potomac to-night,
  Except now and then a stray picket
Is shot, as he walks on his beat to and fro,
  By a rifleman hid in the thicket."
'Tis nothing—a private or two, now and then,
  Will not count in the news of the battle;
Not an officer lost—only one of the men—
  Moaning out, all alone, the death-rattle.

All quiet along the Patomac to-night,
  Where the soldiers lie peacefully dreaming;
Their tents in the rays of the clear autumn moon,
  Or the light of the watch-fires are gleaming.
A tremulous sigh, as the gentle night-wind
  Through the forest leaves slowly is creeping.
While the stars up above, with their glittering eyes,
  Keep guard—for the army is sleeping.

There is only the sound of the lone sentry's tread,
  As he tramps from the rock to the fountain;
And thinks of the two on the low trundle-bed,
  Far away in the cot on the mountain.
His musket falls slack—his face dark and grim,
  Grows gentle with memories tender,
As he mutters a prayer for his children asleep—
  For their mother, may heaven defend Her!

The moon seems to shine as brightly as then,
  That night when the love yet unspoken,
Leaped up to his lips, and when low murmured vows,
  Were pledged to be ever unbroken.
Then drawing his sleeve roughly over his eyes,
  He dashes off tears that are swelling;
And gathers his gun close up to its place,
  As if to keep down the heart-swelling.

He passes the fountain, the blasted pine tree,
  The footstep lagging and weary;
Yet onward he goes, through the broad belt of light,
  Towards the shades of a forest so dreary.
Hark! was it the night-wind that rustled the leaves?
  Was it the moon-light, so wondrously flashing?
It looked like a rifle—ha! Mary, good-bye!
  And the life-blood is ebbing and splashing.

All quiet along the Potomac to-night.
  No sound save the rush of the river;
While soft falls the dew on the face of the dead—
  The picket's off duty forever.

A HYMN

For National Fasting, Humiliation and Prayer.

Prone to the dust, with fear and shame,
  Upon Thy footstool, Lord, we bow:
We glorify Thy holy name,
  And pray for peace and mercy now!

A nation kneels before Thy feet—
  A nation struggling with its foes—
Oh, God of Nations! from Thy seat,
  Look down upon our wants and woes!

Without Thine aid we cannot stand;
  The tyrant will tread down our might;
Oh, Lord, relieve our bleeding land,
  And break the darkness of our night!

We've sent our warriors to the field,
  To meet the vile Philistian horde;
Oh, Father! be to them a shield—
  Oh, give to them the victor's sword!

Our widows weep, our orphans cry,
  Our wives and maidens shrink with fear;
Oh, hear the suffering suppliant's sigh,
  A weak and contrite people hear!

We plead no merit of our own,
  All base and sinful as we are;
We feel we dare not seek Thy throne,
  But with the abject voice of prayer!

Yet Thou didst swear in ancient days,
  That if Thy people would bow down
Thou wouldst forgive their erring ways,
  Nor longer on their efforts frown!

Look then, upon us kneeling now,
  With fasting soul and humble heart;
Oh, from Thy lofty dwelling bow,
  And mercy, grace and strength impart!

Our injured country aid and bless!
  Through war's Red Sea her armies take,
And, safely through the Wilderness,
  Conduct us for Messiah's sake!

GOD OUR REFUGE.

A HYMN.

God is our refuge in this hour
  Of darkness and desmay ;
Our strength against the foeman's power ;
  Our help in battle's day !
Therefore we will not be afraid,
  Though earthquakes shake the ground ;
Though mountains should be level made,
  And waters roar around.

He will his chosen place defend
  Against th' invader's hand:
Their mighty hosts He soon will rend,
  And sweep them from the land !
In vain they form in serried war,
  And wield their flaming swords,—
Jehovah's arm is mightier far,
  To crush their heathen hordes.

He led our fathers thro' the flood
  In freedom's battle morn ;
He blessed the sacrifice of blood,
  When this young land was born ;
To Him in suppliance now we kneel,
  And in His word confide ;
He will, He will His love reveal,
  And safe our armies guide !

Then turn and fly ye heathen host,
    For Jacob's God is here,—
He will deride your haughty boast
    And rend your shaft and spear:
He is our refuge in this hour
    Of darkness and dismay;
Our strength against your pride and power,—
    Our help in battle's day!

A CHANT.

Oft have I seen some sire of Battle's Day,
Whose feet yet lingered on their heavenward way,—
Those feet that tread through Britain's stormy sea,
And gained at length the asylum of the Free,—
Though old and feeble, passionless and lame,
And all unconscious of the voice of Fame,
Yet name the Revolution!—at the word
What proud emotions in his heart are stirred!
His brow grows beautiful!—its seaming scars
Are jewels in the diadem of wars!
How leap his pulses!—in his faded eyes
Gleam the lost splendors of his morning skies.
A youth again—all greedily he hears
The battle trumpet singing in his ears!
His lips grow eloquent—and hark! they tell
The woes and struggles that his youth befell!—
A living history! He proudly boasts
How freedom's sons repelled the tyrant's hosts;

How at Eutaw and Camden, Sumter bled.
And Marion and Pickens bravely led!
Oh! not the blind old bard in Tempe's vale.
More eloquently breathed his battle-tale.
Our Country's ILLIAD from such lips is poured,
While thus they tell the baptism of her sword.

The Last Bugle.

Hark! the muffled drum sounds the last march of the brave,
The soldier retreats to his quarters, the grave,
Under Death, whom he owns his commander in chief,
No more he'll turn out with the ready relief.
But in spite of Death's terrors or hostile alarms,
When he hears the last bugle,
When he hears the last bugle, he'll stand to his arms.

Farewell, brother soldiers, in peace may ye rest,
And light lie the turf on each veteran breast,
Until that review when the souls of the brave
Shall behold the Chief Ensign, fair Mercy's flag, wave:
Then, freed from death's terrors, and hostile alarms,
When we hear the last bugle,
When we hear the last bugle, we'll stand to our arms.

www.ingramcontent.com/pod-product-compliance
Lightning Source LLC
Chambersburg PA
CBHW020146170426
43199CB00010B/912